CLASS AND
PERSONALITY
IN SOCIETY

DISCARD

The Editor

ALAN L. GREY is on the faculty of the Clinical Psychology Program of the Graduate School of Arts and Sciences, Fordham University, where he also has served as a research consultant to the Social Research Institute. He received his B.A. from the City College of the City University of New York, his M.A. from Columbia University, and his Ph.D. from the University of Chicago. He is on the staff of the William Alanson White Institute of Psychoanalysis as a research coordinator and as supervisor of psychotherapy in the Blue Collar Treatment Program of the Low Cost Clinic. Since 1965 he has been a Field Selection Officer for the Peace Corps. In addition to his teaching and research, Dr. Grey is a practicing psychoanalyst and psychotherapist. He has published articles in professional journals and has contributed to several books.

CLASS AND

EDITED BY

Personality in Society

Alan L. Grey

ATHERTON PRESS

New York 1969

Copyright © 1969 by Atherton Press, Inc.

Address all inquiries to:
Atherton Press, Inc.
70 Fifth Avenue
New York 10011

Library of Congress Catalog Card Number 68–56982

FIRST EDITION

Manufactured in the United States of America
DESIGNED BY LORETTA LI

Contents

Introduction

ALAN L. GREY

Class differences, once hidden safely at the back of the American ideological closet, have finally clattered into the political arena to demand recognition. The civil rights movement, Headstart programs, the war on poverty, riot-control legislation, all are separate operations directed toward the same "culturally deprived" people of our nation. As official adoption of that term suggests, the problem is not only financial. Nor is it simply a matter of skin color: hard-core poor whites are involved as well as nonwhites in a multiplicity of legislative plans concerned with so wide a range of ills that plainly the central task is conceived as no less than the revision of total life circumstances for a significant segment of our society.

Whether or not we like the term "class," these limited bits of information about those who are the objects of concern sug-

1

gest that they do constitute a social class—or classes—as defined by the sociologist:

> Social classes may be defined as aggregates of individuals often without specific inherent differentiating characteristics, who enter into and maintain relations with one another on a basis of equality, in contrast to other members of the community from whom they are distinguished (for the moment at least) by socially recognized standards of inferiority and superiority. Members of a given class characteristically develop a similar mode of life and similar attitudes and patterns of behavior and, with varying degrees of explicitness, a sense of belonging together (Alpert, 1964, pp. 56–57).

To the extent that human personality is learned, to the extent that characterological variations are responses to varying life experiences, it becomes plausible to suspect that status differences, and the diversity of circumstances they imply, may also be associated with predictable personality differences. The notion is, of course, not a new one. Aristotle, for instance, put himself on record in behalf of the characterological superiority of the middle classes (Aristotle, in Bendix and Lipset, 1953, pp. 17–18), while the New Testament is well known for its bias in favor of the virtues of the poor. Any literate person can add readily to the list of famous men who made observations about how man's worldly lot may influence his disposition: Machiavelli, Rousseau, Darwin, Marx, Freud, Weber—not to mention a long roster of novelists and other philosophers and scientists—all stated views that have been absorbed into the common opinion that those of the upper classes behave one way and those of the lower classes another (see, for example, Hodges, 1964; Sorokin, 1928). It is to the orderly exploration of this proposition that our attention is directed.

Research in class character covers a range of phenomena that stand at a crossroad between psychology, sociology, psychiatry, anthropology, their sundry subdisciplines, and their intellectual neighbors. A book of this length cannot mirror the full range and depth of thinking on the subject; the plan is, rather, to present some key issues of substance and method via a sampling of articles previously published in the journals of several social sciences. A prime intention in selection was to afford the reader a firsthand experience in examining the divergent ways in which various specialists have viewed and explored the relationship between personality and social status. Hopefully, perusal will offer a sense of how, out of disagreements and confusions, great clarity and sophistication may sometimes emerge. Before turning to the specific papers, a brief review will put the issues into their historical context. An accompanying bibliography allows for further pursuit of facets which may prove interesting.

MODERN BEGINNINGS: PERSONALITY UNDIFFERENTIATED FROM CULTURE

In contemporary history there are at least three related social-science specialties concerned with the interplay between environment and individual characteristics: personality-and-culture, national-character, and class-character research. Since all are involved in the quest for a conceptual system to adequately explain the interaction between social circumstances and individual response patterns, any development in social theory, in personality formulations, or in research methods useful in any one of these fields has usually found its way into the others. Thus, a sound perspective on class-character research calls for some consideration of all three areas and, in fact, of the broader fields from which they have emerged.

During the first part of the twentieth century, social science was profoundly stirred by the anthropologists' new concept of culture and its implications, for their study of exotic societies seriously challenged prevailing notions that there can be absolute standards of what is right or wrong. Where preliterate peoples had once been regarded as "primitive" and inferior to ourselves, anthropologists questioned such views as ethnocentric. They spoke of a principle of cultural relativity according to which "good" and "bad" are meaningful only in the context of a particular civilization. The eloquent words of a later commentator, Lawrence Frank (1948), express the heady ambiance of a cultural determinism espoused by many social anthropologists:

> In the years to come it is possible that this discovery of the human origin and development of culture will be recognized as the greatest of all discoveries, since heretofore man has been helpless before these cultural and social formulations which generation after generation have perpetuated the same frustration and defeat of human values and aspirations. . . . Now man is beginning to realize that his culture and social organization are not unchanged cosmic processes but are human creations which may be altered.

Ideas of this sort made it inevitable that social scientists of the nineteen twenties and thirties would consider the most intimate aspects of human personality as likely to be shaped to the social milieu. Their investigations, however, met with difficulties that can be illustrated by considering the views of Edward Sapir, one of the most influential anthropologists during the decades after World War I. A quotation from one of his essays reflects the manifold meanings assigned to the term "culture" during those years:

> The word "culture" seems to be used in three main senses or groups of senses. First of all, culture is technically used by the ethnologist and culture historian to embody any socially inherited element in the life of man, material and spiritual. Culture so defined is coterminous with man himself, for even the lowliest savage lives in a complex network of traditionally conserved habits, usages and attitudes. . . . The second application of the term . . . refers . . . to a rather conventional ideal of individual refinement. . . . In brief, this cultured ideal is a vesture and an air. The third use . . . aims to embrace in a single term those general attitudes, views of life and specific manifestations of civilization that give a particular people its distinctive place in the world. . . . Culture, then, may be briefly defined as civilization insofar as it embodies the national genius . . . (Sapir, 1924).

Obviously, much of what Sapir calls "culture" might also be regarded as "personality" as the word is used today. When a year after these remarks one of Sapir's students, Leslie A. White, published a paper whose title, "Personality and Culture" (Kluckhohn *et al.,* 1953), stuck as a label for the new field, part of the heritage of the term was a continuing fuzziness in identifying which phenomena are "culture" and which are "personality." Since both are abstractions referring to different aspects of the same phenomena—the behavior of individual human beings—the overlap is understandable. Unfortunately, this state of affairs can hamper research, for it does not provide for separate observation of the two relevant variables. Thus, any relationship found may be merely an artifact of the definition of terms.

Exactly such criticisms were leveled at what generally is regarded as the first major work produced in "personality and culture": Ruth Benedict's *Patterns of Culture* (1934). A persuasive depiction of how human nature is molded by society in several preliterate groups, it might equally well have been called "Patterns of Personality," for it used the same concepts and data almost interchangeably to examine both customs and character. In fairness, however, this defect was not peculiar to gifted ethnologists like Sapir and Benedict; it reflected, rather, theoretical difficulties prevalent at the time, for setting up clear, operational definitions for personality variables was a thorny problem. So thorny a problem that an important group of ethnologists, including men of the caliber of Franz Boas, were inclined to bypass the study of personality entirely, for they were skeptical that scientifically satisfactory solutions of the methodological problems could be found (see, for example, Kardiner and Preble, 1963).

FREUD FILLS THE VACUUM

Clearly, the dilemma facing early students of personality and culture was formidable. In the absence of academically respectable tools for investigating the individual there seemed little choice but to avoid the endeavor or, like Benedict, to muddle through with literary improvisations.

For Bronislaw Malinowski, however, neither alternative was acceptable. He saw the description of physical objects of the "material culture" apart from an understanding of their personal meaning as a waste of time, for the significance of any object, he thought, must lie precisely in its function for the user. One had to grasp the native's point of view, his orientation to living, *his* vision of *his* world. If the academicians could not provide means for accomplishing this, he saw a better solution than Benedict's amateur psychologizing: The alternative was to go outside conventional academic boundaries to the ideas of a highly original expert on personality who was attracting increasing attention. Sigmund Freud and his followers had developed a theory based on extensive clinical observation that appeared to unlock the mystery behind rather puzzling facets of human behavior. Finding it directed at the same goal as his own research—the understanding of subjective meanings and their place in the total life experience of the human animal—Malinowski introduced psychoanalytic theory to the anthropologists, many of whom went on to exercise important influence both within their own field and within the other social sciences: Mead, DuBois, Bateson, Linton, Kluckhohn, to mention but a few.

Even Malinowski, however, was by no means an uncritical disciple of Freud. He went into some detail to point out, for instance, that the alleged universality of the Oedipus complex was an ethnographic error, contradicted by his own observations of the Trobriand Islanders (1927). His skepticism was shared by numerous other anthropologists. Among them was Kluckhohn, who, in his own excellent review of the subject (1954), nicely reflects the mixture of criticism and appreciation that has characterized ethnographers' reactions to psychoanalysis. On the one hand, he dismisses the psychoanalysts:

How helpful the suggestions of Freud, Roheim, and Kardiner are is arguable. Freud's "Just So Stories" are contradicted, at least in detail, by much ethnographic evidence (p. 961).

But on the other, he clarifies the methodological adaptability of psychoanalysis in this fashion:

> . . . the dominant experience of cultural anthropologists had been "unscientific"—in the narrow sense of that term—as that of the psychoanalysts. Both groups operate with procedures that are essentially "clinical." Ordinarily the anthropologist working under field conditions has as little chance to do controlled experiments as has the psychoanalyst who sees his patient for an hour a day in the consulting room. The skilled of both professions do make predictions of a crude order and test them by subsequent observation. But these observations do not lend themselves to presentation in neat graphs nor to "t" tests (p. 964).

PROBLEMS OF METHOD

The thrust of Kluckhohn's criticism reflects a characteristic problem of the culture-personality tradition. Like psychoanalysis, it has been most concerned with *in vivo* observations about human nature and far less with niceties of method; and, like psychoanalysis, it has been criticized particularly for its use of "clinical-idiosyncratic" research procedures (Inkeles and Levinson, 1954, p. 988). The chief methodological faults associated with this area might be grouped under two headings: first, the tendency toward looseness in basic conceptualization, and second, a lack of objective rigor in data collection.

Thus, on the first score, anthropologists using psychoanalytic theory have tended to cull together data on an intuitive basis without following theories systematically and without explicitly stating their own modifications. As one can see from the earlier papers in this volume, this looseness of design was carried from the parent field into the early life of its offspring, class-character relations. Havighurst and Davis (1955), for instance, or White (1957), are notably vague about just what kind of parental training leads to which sort of child character. They are especially fuzzy about providing factual data concerning the offspring that would confirm or deny their hypotheses about home influences. The earlier anthropological works are even more remiss in this respect. They usually offer no fixed schedule of evidence collected and no control data against which postulated relationships might be tested. A researcher who has strong feelings that toilet training, for instance, is very influential in shaping personality patterns in a particular society might present the evidence for his case but give little or no information about other early experiences (see, for example, Gorer, 1948). Since he has employed the Freudian theory of psychosexual development, he provides, at best, a very incomplete report of the various stages; in effect, such work constitutes the defense of his propositions rather than a test of them.

The second methodological defect, unreliability in factual observations, becomes obvious when the same society is described quite differently by various ethnographers. During the early decades of this century, there was great pressure to have at least one report of each culture before it was engulfed in the spread of Western civilization. Thus, replicative studies seldom occurred. More recently, however, as they have become feasible, additional studies of an area have led to some classic instances of disagreement between reputable anthropologists. When Lewis (1951) studied the Mexican village of Tepoztlán, previously described in a notable work by Redfield (1946), he found their impressions almost diametrically opposed. As Lewis put it, Redfield had seen "a relatively homogeneous, isolated, smoothly functioning and well-integrated society," while he himself found "a lack of cooperation . . . and the pervading quality of fear, envy and distrust in interpersonal relations."

This particular difficulty has proven much less formidable in today's replicative social-character research, for one of the clearest trends, reflected in the series of papers following, is a progressive sharpening of research questions and design. This is due in part to the invasion of the field by increasing numbers of sociologists and social psychologists who have brought systematic and quantitative research methods from their own disciplines. Conflicting reports are still possible, as Havighurst and Davis indicate in their United States study in this book; yet the discrepancies are less gross and more readily resolvable with systematic research, as Mary White's paper, also reprinted here, reflects. And too, psychologists have brought tighter research designs to their own investigations of child-rearing practices in exotic cultures, as in the work of J. W. M. Whiting and I. L. Child (1953) and their associates (Beatrice Whiting, 1963; Minturn and Lambert, 1964). Certainly in the last decade, then, the study of interaction between social environment and personality has moved away from its earlier impressionistic style and into the methodological mainstream of social science.

The specific references here are, of course, only a meager indication of the extent of work in personality and culture and its overlapping sister discipline, national character. Since the beginning of World War II in particular, political events have led to a great flowering of activity in these fields, and interested readers are referred to the extensive selected bibliography (988 references) on *National Character and National Stereotypes* (1960) provided by Duijker and Frijda under the auspices of the International Committee for Social Science Documentation of the United Nations.

THE POSITIVE LEGACY OF PSYCHOANALYTIC-ETHNOGRAPHIC COLLABORATION

The strong interest in socialization that has persisted in personality-culture, national-character, and class-character research is, obviously, inherited from psychoanalytic theory, whose core orientation is the interaction between biological growth and life experiences during the time from birth to puberty. The theory of psychosexual stages, the structure and typology of personality, thought processes and defenses, all are related to this central theme, which, translated into the language of the sociologist, becomes the "socialization experience," that wide range of subprocesses, particularly child-rearing practices, by which an individual learns the cultural system of the society to which he belongs. As is often the case with complex ideas, "socialization" has been variously understood. It is often used to connote conformity, for instance, suggesting that insofar as one deviates from convention he is "unsocialized" (see Child, 1954, p. 655). A judgmental and unnecessary limitation in the eyes of this psychologist, who would see "deviational" behavior as similar to conformist behavior in that it is a learned response to social experience and based on the same psychological processes.

However, despite terminological variations, and despite the failure of specific aspects of Freud's system to stand the test of scientific research, there is no question that he deserves credit for having generated a major theme of fruitful inquiry. Of the eight papers in the collection following, more than half are directly concerned with socialization processes, a proportion entirely in line with the general trend. Only in recent years have alternative explanations of the persistence of behavior been offered in sufficient strength to draw attention away from the socialization theory. These recent formulations, like those of the Pearlin and Kohn study in this collection, emphasize the influence of the current life situation of the individual rather than his past. In the long run, however, research is likely to prove that such factors are covariables with, rather than successors to, historical explanations.

But the borrowing of ideas has not by any means been a one-sided process, with anthropology as passive recipient. By the middle 1930's a number of psychoanalysts, profoundly affected by the implications of comparative cultural data, departed from Freudian orthodoxy. In *Psychoanalysis: Evaluation and Development* (1950), Clara Thompson, a leading member of the neo-Freudian revolution, refers to Edward Sapir and Ruth Benedict as ethnographers who were particularly influential among the dissident psychoanalysts, one of whom, Dr. Abram Kardiner, collaborated with anthropologist Ralph Linton in the writing of *The Individual and His Society* (1939).

While not breaking with Freud officially, he revised a number of classic ideas heavily enough to displease his colleagues and too lightly to satisfy social scientists—but enough to improve the level of previous work.

Perhaps even better known were three analysts who went beyond Kardiner and dared to break openly with official psychoanalysis on the strength of social science re-formulations. Karen Horney, Harry Stack Sullivan, and Erich Fromm might claim the distinction of being first to put culture-personality research to practical applications in their revisions of psychoanalytic ideas and treatment methods. Their roots in social science make these neo-Freudians distinctly different from the other dissidents with whom their names are often erroneously linked: Rank and Jung. These last names are closer perhaps to contemporary "ego psychology" in rejecting the reductionism of early psychoanalysis, which tended to emphasize intrapsychic processes to the neglect of the external world. In the view of this latter group, human actions are related to an external environment, which is largely a cultural product but one whose realities must be understood by the psychotherapist. Their theories provide a springboard for such important psychiatric innovations as community psychiatry and the social study of class differences between patients (see the paper by Grey in this volume).

From among the neo-Freudians, however, there also emerged a study of particular importance to our discussion here— Erich Fromm's *Escape from Freedom* (1941), a brilliant analysis that points to the personality structure of the lower-middle classes as a crucial factor in Germany's acceptance of National Socialism. The "authoritarian character" syndrome Fromm discusses was a re-casting of the classic psychoanalytic notion of sado-masochism in terms of his own neo-Freudian sociology. As Fromm explains it:

> Since the term "sado-masochistic" is associated with perversion and neurosis, I prefer to speak of the sado-masochistic character, especially when not the neurotic but the normal person is meant, as the "authoritarian character". . . . He admires authority and

tends to submit to it, but at the same time he wants to be an authority himself and have others submit to him (p. 164).

The authoritarian personality type has continued to receive considerable attention since 1941. It was investigated systematically by Adorno and his associates (1950), and together they also developed psychometric scales for its measurement. Their basic formulation has stood up very well (Brown, 1965, pp. 477–546; Samelson and Yates, 1967) even under the searching eye of many subsequent reviewers (see, for example, Christie and Jahoda, 1954). Some facets of the study have undergone further development by other investigators, one such theme being the degree to which authoritarianism varies with social status. Explicitly or otherwise, a number of class-character studies have been concerned with this question. The sustained interest it has received is more than a matter of mere fashion or chance, for the organization of power is an aspect of all social life and all individuals in social groups must, in some fashion or other, come to terms with the exercise of authority. Indeed, an attempt to identify standard issues that could provide a basis for comparison of personality types across cultures led Inkeles and Levinson to assert that "The issue *relation to authority* meets our criteria of universal psychosocial relevance" (1954, p. 990). It is, in fact, the common theme with which all the papers in this collection are concerned.

The description of a single personality type like authoritarianism obviously does not resolve all the knotty problems encountered in culture-personality research. Syndrome X may apply to Culture X but be useless in the description of Society Y. And, as any field study reveals, even in the simplest tribe one standard pattern fits very few members exactly and some not at all. Obviously, then, as the investigator moves from a preliterate group to a complex culture, the difficulties of pattern formulations will multiply. In *Escape from Freedom,* Fromm himself was among the first to offer a solution to this dilemma with the notion of "social character."

The social character comprises only a selection of traits, the essential nucleus of the character structure of most members of a group which has developed as the result of the basic experiences and modes of life common to that group (p. 277). . . . Different societies of classes within a society have a specific social character (p. 279).

Escape from Freedom was more successful than previous works had been in treating personality and social institutions as separate variables without resorting to the use of either one as a monistic determinant of historical events; and yet, despite Fromm's skillful integration of psychoanalysis and sociology, his own ideas were not widely influential in the social sciences. Some may have been affected negatively by the increasingly moralistic tone of his subsequent works (Schaar, 1961), but perhaps more important was the general academic resistance to psychoanalytic thought, and, among an important segment of social scientists, the rejection of any consideration of the psychological. Excepting of course those anthropologists who drew on Freud, the generalization is a valid one: an overview of *Sociology Today* published in 1959 finds Inkeles still protesting the "attempt to analyze social phenomena with a method which strictly excludes psychological theory and data" (p. 249). (It is this which may also explain why Anderson's pioneering work on class variations in child-rearing practices was largely overlooked by sociologists when it appeared in 1936, even though it was based on a national sample, sound statistical analysis, and sponsored by the White House Conference on Child Health and Protection.)

Although the class-character studies collected here reflect a progressive advance in research design, they make no notable improvement on Fromm's basic conceptualization—which is not to dismiss the accumulated efforts of several decades but to clarify the nature of the accomplishment. Together, the papers here represent the scientific implementation of an idea derived from psychoanalysis, an implementation that has been crucial in establishing the validity of certain hypotheses, in making specific aspects more explicit—and, finally, in battering down some of the academic resistance to psychoanalytic-based theory.

THE BEGINNINGS OF CLASS-CHARACTER RESEARCH

Indeed, it might be said that class-character research was one of the back doors through which Freud slipped into the sociological imagination. Among those who opened the door was John Dollard, whose own training drew from sociology, anthropology, psychoanalysis, and learning theory. He had helped Edward Sapir at Yale to lead the first formal culture-and-personality seminar in 1932 and so had been in on the ground floor—where the back doors are usually located. The titles of some of his earlier books—*Criteria for the Life History* (1935), *Caste and Class in a Southern Town* (1937), and, in collaboration with Allison Davis, *Children of Bondage* (1940)—reflect his interest in systematizing the use of biographical data for research purposes. They also indicate the pursuit of a major theme, an effort to understand how status institutions have affected the character not only of the Negro in the United States but of his white superordinates as well.

Drawing on the psychoanalytic tradition, the 1937 volume included dreams and jokes as part of its data and offered essentially psychodynamic explanations of the personality processes involved; but Dollard has also done much to reconcile psychoanalysis with more explicit and experimentally operational learning theory (1939, 1950). This interest is reflected in *Children of Bondage,* which attempts "to recreate the personalities and to describe the socialization of eight Negro adolescents in the Deep South of this country" (p. xix). Although a sample of 123 children and their parents was used for background information, the study concentrates on the eight biographies, each regarded as typical, or "modal," for a given Negro social class position—that is, a subdivision of lower, middle, or upper class within the Negro caste. The report eschewed the statistical tables characteristic of many recent sociological papers of this genre—the collection in this volume for instance—perhaps because tabular material seemed less communicative of the interpersonal interactions that concerned the authors. Their underlying theory is quoted here as a succinct statement of what is also a current viewpoint:

> . . . the conditions under which persons have access to fundamental biological and social goals are defined by a system of privilege. When this system is examined in detail, as it recently has been studied in New England and in the lower South by social anthropologists who lived in these communities for extended periods, it is found to be a system of socially ranked groups, with varying degrees of social movement existing between them. . . . In our society, an individual is born into a family which is a member of such a socially ranked group. His family's economic, social and sexual participation is largely limited to its own group. He is controlled by his social position, not simply in the formation of his early habits, but throughout his life. He is controlled by the punishment which he receives from groups above and below him to restrict his participation, that is, to "keep him in his (social) place." The effect of such punishment is usually to prevent him from learning new habits, and thus from increasing his privileges. Barriers upon interclass participation thus set up differential reinforcements for each group; the nature of these social reinforcements is ultimately determined by the kind of privileges (goal responses) which the group is allowed to attain (pp. 11–12).

The stratification system referred to is W. Lloyd Warner's, who in 1941, and in collaboration with Lunt, published *The Social Life of a Modern Community*, which describes what has been dubbed the "Pullman System" of class divisions. These include upper upper (UU), lower upper (LU), upper middle (UM), lower middle (LM), upper lower (UL), and lower lower (LL), position being determined by Warner's "Index of Status Characteristics" whereby a score is derived from a suitable combination of seven scales rating such personal characteristics as occupation, income, education, residence, religion, and so forth. Despite subsequent criticisms, Warner's device spurred on class-character research. "Few multiple item measures have been more cautiously constructed and so frequently used," wrote Hodges (1964, p. 96), and Warner's work was duly acknowledged in *Children of Bondage*: "For the conception that social class and caste form the underlying structure of Southern society and for theoretical application of this problem to personality typing, the authors are indebted to F. Lloyd Warner of the University of Chicago" (p. xii).

But, beyond its integration of a new stratification system, the statement itself is an integration of situational and psychological variables. And in its use of terms like "punishment," "habit," and "reinforcement," it also exemplifies an interesting process in the sociology of ideas. It shows how men like Dollard, influenced by both psychoanalysis and learning theory, have facilitated the ingestion into social psychology of insights from distastefully unscientific psychoanalysis (see also Janis *et al.*, 1959, and Pitts, 1961, pp. 690*ff*.). The process, at its best, is one of the creative translation of psychoanalytic language into something more palatable and operational, an Americanization process, which, if it succeeds, may produce a more colorless but certainly more universally acceptable system that draws strengths from both clinical and academic traditions. The previously cited work of Whiting and Child, of Adorno *et al.*, and, in sociology, of Parsons and Shils (1951), Gerth and Mills (1953), all reflect this trend in their various ways.

Among the personality concepts used in class-character research today, variants of "derived psychoanalysis" are most influential. Although their link with Freud may be somewhat obscured by modifications of language, the link exists insofar as one regards the investigation of socialization, a concern with defensive mechanisms, or the use of characterological labels like "authoritarianism" as having some roots in Vienna. Even in the development of something so specific as the F scale by Adorno *et al.*, items for the detection of authoritarianism were phrased to reflect relevant "orality and anality" (pp. 445*ff*). Sometimes, of course, the approach exceeds the understanding of the psychoanalytic principle, and sometimes the principle is used as casually as it was by ethnologists in the past. But at its best in a blend with a sound learning theory, with a valid research design, or, as in the papers in this collection, with considerable quantitative precision and testability, the derived psychoanalytic proposition may well be improved by its new rigor.

The Chicago Group

With Warner and Davis both at the University of Chicago, that institution had an excellent nucleus for further ventures into class-character territory, and a number of studies came forth. They began with Warner's "Yankee City" series (1941, 1942, 1945, 1947), each written with a collaborator who went on to make his own contributions. Davis, who had collaborated with Dollard on *Children of Bondage* and with the Gardners on *Deep South* (1941), also wrote *Social-Class Influences upon Learning* (1949), which explored the relationship between class and the educational system. It dealt with a concern that also led to Davis' work on "culture fair" tests. As a graduate student at Chicago, I was led by similar thinking about the middle-class orientation in psychiatry to dissertation research in 1949 that anticipated much of Hollingshead and Redlich's New Haven study (1958).

Of particular interest to us, however, is the Chicago Ph.D. thesis by Martha Ericson, reported in an article she wrote in 1946. It was part of a larger study by Havighurst and Davis that they first described in a 1946 paper, "Social Class and Color Differences in Child Rearing," and in a book the following year. Their study was important not only for its findings but because they also captured the attention of American social psychologists and stimulated a great series of studies and productive controversies in the class-character field. In the words of Bronfenbrenner (1958):

> During the past dozen years, a class struggle has been taking place in American social psychology—a struggle, fortunately, not *between* but *about* social classes. . . . [It] reached a climax in 1946 with the publication of Davis and Havighurst's influen-

tial paper on "Social Class and Color Differences in Child Rearing." The paper cited impressive statistical evidence in support of the thesis that middle-class parents "place their children under a stricter regime, with more frustration of their impulses than do lower class parents." For the next eight years, the Davis-Havighurst conclusion was taken as the definitive statement of class differences in socialization. Then, in 1954, came the counterrevolution; Maccoby and Gibbs published the first report of a study of child-rearing practices in the Boston area which, by and large, contradicted the Chicago findings. . . . In response, one year later, Havighurst and Davis presented a re-analysis of their data. . . .

The controversy launched by Davis and Havighurst is the specific point of departure for the papers collected in this volume, all of which deal with issues triggered by the Chicago-Boston contradictions. Special attention is due Warner and his associates in this connection because their work, insofar as it deals with the fundamental issue, is relevant to all other investigations of class and character. That is, it provides functional answers to the problems of how to describe the status structure of a modern community and how to identify the position in it of specific individuals.

Others, before and since the University of Chicago group, have made influential contributions in these matters. Some of these studies are not reported because they are tangential to our prime focus; others are passed over when they are considered in one or another of the reprinted articles. But this still leaves a considerable body of thought about the nature of prestige systems, to which we shall now turn our attention.

THEORIES OF SOCIAL CLASS AND STATUS INDICES

Sociologists are by no means agreed about the precise form of the central status structure of the United States, nor about the most suitable instrument for identifying the position of a particular individual within it. But there is sufficient consensus so that measurement devices correlate with each other fairly well.

A very simple approach, one that has occurred to many, was provided as long ago as the third century B.C., when Aristotle divided the social strata of the state into "three elements: one class is very rich, another very poor, and a third is a mean" (1953, p. 17). Following his lead, one might specify class limits in precise, quantitative terms of income. This procedure, however, has both practical and theoretical disadvantages: many an opinion poll interviewer, for instance, has discovered that it is easier to induce a respondent to disclose his sexual activities than his income. And even if the information were obtainable it still might be quite misleading: a thief or a prostitute might earn more than a clergyman or teacher and yet is not of a higher class, as the idea generally is understood.

A more sophisticated but still "materialist" definition is Karl Marx's identification of class in terms of one's relation to the means of production. "To be a capitalist is to have not only a purely personal, but a social status interest in production" (1932, p. 336). His theory, in fact, related economic role to total personality: "Does it require deep intuition to comprehend that man's ideas, views and conceptions, in one word, man's consciousness, changes with every change in the conditions of his material existence, in his social relations and in his social life?" Marx asked (p. 341). This view, less simply materialistic than its popular reputation might suggest, lends itself readily to class-character theory.

Many American sociologists have ignored or challenged the Marxian formulation in their own discussions of social class. Nuances of theory significant to the specialist are beyond our immediate interest, but interested readers can find summaries of different views in more specialized books on social stratification (see, for example, Page, 1940, for earlier views, and Hodges, 1964, for more recent ones). What most of these American thinkers share is the notion that a cornerstone of class or status is the factor of relative prestige. But, since they do not see class differences as an inevitable source of strong class antagonism, in this, and in certain other respects, they are closer to the tradition of Max Weber (Weber, 1947, pp. 424–

429) than to that of Marx. Lloyd Warner, for instance, saw persuasive evidence for a shift from a Marxist orientation to the more typical American "multifactor" approach emphasizing prestige (Kornhauser, 1953, p. 226).

More informative than definitions alone, however, are the various operational indices of class developed, among others, by Warner, Hollingshead and Redlich, North and Hatt, and Hodges. The facts of our class system as they emerge from the empirical inquiries using operational measures indicate that at any given prestige level there tends to be a clustering of numerous personality similarities, thus confirming the view that status is associated with a whole way of living. A list, by no means exhaustive, of status-related characteristics would include type of occupation, patterns of social participation, income, education, residence type and location, tastes and values, illness and mortality rates, and religion and ethnic origin. The situation has been summed up in these words: "Socioeconomic status has been a variable in countless studies, almost always a useful one, as there is not much in human behavior that is completely independent of status" (Brown, 1965, p. 149).

Thus, a wide variety of criteria—even one's living room furniture (Chapin, 1928)—prove useful clues to social position. Different researchers have preferred various devices for their own particular purposes; yet the correlation between their several procedures has resulted in mutually relevant findings, even in the absence of complete agreement about the "true" nature of social class. The situation resembles that in the field of intelligence testing where debate continues about the "real" meaning of the intelligence concept, but where the mutually correlated, predictively useful devices nevertheless afford a pool of useful information.

For all its advantages, however, such a state of affairs is not ideal. The very temptation to equate findings derived from different status measures is bound to lead to contradictions and confusions about research data. At what level does the "lower class" begin and how does it differ from the "working class" or the "blue collar" class? How does one calibrate the occupational measure of another researcher, or check the consistency of results? A classic instance of the difficulties in comparing socialization studies is provided by Bronfenbrenner (1958). Despite the fact that most of the projects he examined were based on criteria derived from Warner, numerous adjustments in status boundaries were necessary before he could make direct comparisons of associated social behavior.

Kahl and Davis (1955) are among other researchers who have sought to reduce ambiguity by determining which single variable is most highly predictive across a wide range of social behavior. In their study, factor analysis indicated occupation as the one most useful criterion for the American scene, a finding that not only rests on purely empirical evidence, but is also consistent with a widely recognized sociological formulation of American class structure. Talcott Parsons, for instance, sees "our central status system" as based on "occupational roles" (1953, p. 115). And, it is interesting to note that while Marx proceeded from an economic reference point and American sociologists from culture values, there are instances when both converge operationally on occupation as the key to individual prestige, power, and life style.

How Well Do Indices Predict Realities?

Despite these impressive accumulations of evidence, social psychologist Roger Brown has been among a number of thinkers who have seriously questioned the reality of social classes. Brown does not challenge the right or wisdom of an investigator in setting up statistical "classes" or interval limits to investigate correlations between prestige and other characteristics. But, as he states his case:

> Imposed classes which do not pretend to be descriptions of an underlying social reality had best be called categorizations. . . . The reality of a class in a community will be undeniable in the following circumstances: (1) the population is conscious of

classes, agreed on the number of classes, and on the member-ship of them; (2) styles of life are strikingly uniform within a stratum and there are clear contrasts between strata; (3) inter-action is sharply patterned by stratum; (4) the boundaries are conditions to which caste-structured societies approximate but the conditions are logically independent of mobility and could obtain without rigidity of boundaries. In the degree that the conditions listed are not satisfied, the reality of class becomes doubtful (1965, p. 134).

In applying the first criterion, Brown finds that the United States does not fulfill the characteristics of a class system, basing his case on the well-attested fact that Americans are notoriously reluctant to show any open class consciousness (see, for ex-ample, Hodges, 1964, pp. 1–16). Even sociologists have tended to see classlessness in the American scene until recent decades (Page, 1940, p. 250). Centers (1949) has been particularly vehement in asserting the meaninglessness of discussing a social class unless its alleged members are aware of belonging to it. But this position is by no means unchallenged (e.g., Hodges, 1964, pp. 87*ff*), for the fact that many do not use the word class in describing themselves, or use it inaccurately, does not preclude their exclusion of others from their offices, social clubs, or homes—with some other euphemism employed in explana-tion. In these days of sophisticated semantics and dissociative phenomena, the fact that a particular culturally disapproved word is not used is not very weighty evidence to refute the ex-tensive documentation of selective social participation (Warner, 1949; Hollingshead, 1949; Kahl and Davis, 1955). In short, status indices predict social clusterings independently of what people may publicly state.

Brown's second stipulation has special relevance for our cen-tral focus inasmuch as style of life is a salient expression of personality. If particular character types are associated with specific class levels, then each level should manifest its own distinctive values and behavior. And, as Brown himself notes, "There is very little in life that does not vary at least prob-abilistically with social standing" (1965, p. 132). It is also true, however, that the precise prestige level at which any given kind of behavior changes is often not identical with the cutoff point for another activity. This overlap has led experts to disagree about the exact boundaries of a class, as well as about the number and identity of strata in the total social system (see, e.g., Cohen and Riessman this volume).

Proceeding, now, to Brown's third criterion: patterns of interaction have, in fact, shown definite stratum clusterings in the United States, and, as has already been mentioned, what may appear to be spontaneous choice of one's associates is reasonably predictable from prestige measures. Once it is recognized that actual social participation is at least as significant a sign of class consciousness as verbal behavior, Brown's first measure —"class consciousness"—and his third cannot be separated functionally as well as they can logically, for the evidence suggests that on the American scene at least, class consciousness is reflected more clearly in actions than in words. Obviously, class consciousness in Karl Marx's sense of group identity for mass revolutionary action is not the only kind of status awareness which can preserve prestige systems, for there is also the "gentleman's agreement," often unspoken, to include these people and exclude those. Social psychologists inadvertently limit themselves, however, to a Marxian viewpoint when they require explicit declarations of class affiliation as essential marks of a class system.

While graduations of interaction can be observed, their boundaries in the social system are blurred: those for any one characteristic—occupational level, for instance—are not precisely coincident with others—income, for instance, education, neighborhood. Thus, Brown's third and fourth criteria are not fully satisfied. If all four standards had been fully met, it would indicate that the United States has either a caste system or what sociologists (see, for example, MacIver, 1931) have long called a "corporate class system." When Brown concludes, as he does, that classes are not "real" in the sense of his definition, he is in substantial agreement with most sociologists, who also assert that our country is not primarily a caste or corporate class system. For example, consider Leonard Broom's report in *Sociology Today* (1959):

> With few exceptions, American researchers have been reluctant to accept *a priori* and have been unable to discover empirically the reality of class in the sense of fully developed, sharply defined strata comprised of individuals who are aware of their positions and capable of corporate action. The inference of class from a single psychological property or attitude in a delimited sphere of interest is, of course, inadmissible (p. 435).

THE COMPETITIVE CLASS SYSTEM

How can such conclusions, which seem to dismiss the significance of social class in American life, be reconciled with previously cited facts to the contrary? The answer is that while "class," insofar as it implies open recognition of one's position, is not aptly descriptive of a large part of our status system, behavior does indicate status gradations, which Americans are simply loath to acknowledge. For these status gradations, which do have a measurable impact on our life patterns and opportunities, Brown proposes the term "continuum of socioeconomic status," another label for the "competitive class system."

The competitive class system refers to a series of subtle gradations in prestige and life circumstances that may have a wide range but wherein any two adjacent levels may overlap considerably. Typically, people who live within such a system aspire to rise in the world on the basis of their individual competitive efforts rather than via group loyalties and cooperation. A cohesive sense of class identity ("corporate class consciousness") in nineteenth-century Europe led men like Karl Marx to foresee the possibility of a corporate revolutionary action, a class struggle causing the overthrow of existing elites. That increasing means of production might lead to changed patterns of distribution, with an increasing abundance of bread and circuses for the great masses, was not a possibility anticipated by Marx and Engels. This spreading of material comforts brings some prognosticators to envision the United States as a "national society" with "the rise of mass production and mass consumption and the consequent leveling of distinctive class styles of life" (Bell, 1962, p. 7).

As matters stand now, it must be recognized that the United States is somewhat short of universal affluence, whether or not such a state is our future. Indeed, certain parts of our social system, particularly the submerged non-whites, have been partitioned off with sharp and by now highly visible barriers. And, in white society, a hard-core segment with its own typical behavior system remains in a state of poverty while, at the upper extreme, distinct demarcations are observable between "old family" elites and achievement elites. Here again, however, experts disagree about certain details: Parsons, for instance (1953, p. 123), is doubtful about whether the old aristocracy is as influential as Warner portrays it. Thus, rather than a simple continuum, the American structure is partly a caste system (racially), partly a corporate class system (at both extremes of the white caste), with an extensive competitive class system between these poles. As Marx would have predicted, class conflict does occur, particularly in those parts of the system where status barriers are most fixed.

Not surprisingly then, the status structure of our complex nation is a rather complex affair. To complicate it further, there are continual changes with time, as Mary White (1957) points out in the paper included here. The social psychologist using status measures needs to be informed not only about matters psychological but also about nuances of the social and political circumstances to which his subjects are responding. All too often, psychologists treat the numerical scores of the status indicator as if they report uniform, quantitative units that distinguish equal differences at all points of their range. The fact is that a few units of difference may be associated with considerable divergences in life style at lower and upper ends of a particular scale while larger differences in the middle may signify far less. As Miller and Riessman (1961) clearly state in the article reprinted in this volume, such naiveté has some-times led to spurious interpretations of findings and unneces-sary controversy. Whether or not it has been of any comfort to psychologists, they have been able to point to their socio-logical colleagues' similar blind spots about the personality formulations to which we now turn our attention.

Role Theory: Conceptual Link Between Society and Individual

A central question of class-character research is whether the occupants of a given status show regularities in their social behavior that distinguish them from the occupants of other positions in the same society. Although our brief review of status systems has indicated that such regularities do occur, it still leaves unanswered the questions about the extent of these regularities and the specific ways in which they come about. Sociologists have long been concerned with these matters. Among those who have attempted to construct a comprehen-sive theory of human behavior, none has received more respect-ful attention than Talcott Parsons and Edward Shils and a distinguished roster of their collaborators—E. C. Tolman, G. W. Allport, C. Kluckhohn, H. A. Murray, R. R. Sears, R. C. Shel-don, and S. A. Stouffer. In their 1951 statement, *Toward a General Theory of Action*, Parsons and Shils offer three con-cepts as the cornerstones of their system: "personality," or the individual's organization of his biological and experiential heri-tage; "social system," or the ongoing social relationships and situations which affect him; and "culture," or the values and orientations to which he has been exposed and which Kluck-hohn has called "the precipitate of history" (1954, p. 922).

Additional concepts are introduced to explain the mediating processes through which, for instance, personality is influenced by the social system or the social system is perpetuated in the behavior of individuals. Perhaps most important of these explanatory ideas is "role."

> For most analytical purposes, the most significant unit of social structures is not the person but the role. The role is that organized sector of an actor's orientation which constitutes and defines his participation in an interactive process. . . . Roles are institutionalized when they are fully congruous with the prevailing culture patterns and are organized around expectations of conformity with morally sanctioned patterns of value orientation shared by the members of the collectivity in which the role functions (Parsons and Shils, 1951, p. 23).

Within the framework of our concern here, "role" might be defined as the behavior one is expected to manifest as the occupant of a particular status situation in the social system. To take an obvious example: In the role of physician, one is expected to respond differently to the sight of a nude body than in the role of lover. Role expectations will, of course, vary— even for the same role—with time, place, and the particular significance of the role. Thus, although the role of the priest is less strictly codified than it was fifty years ago, it is still more elaborately defined than that of the postman, and, in that it covers more than his specifically clerical functions, it is more *extensively* codified, for it covers his dress, speech, and response to women in a social situation.

The term itself was originally introduced to social science by Ralph Linton in his *Study of Man* (1936), and role theorists, beginning with Linton, have always been careful to distinguish between "role" and "personality." As Linton himself put it:

> The status personality does not correspond to the total personality but simply to certain aspects . . . of the latter, i.e., to those elements of the total personality which are immediately concerned with the performance of the individual's roles. There can be no doubt that certain psychological types are better adapted to particular status personalities than others, but individuals of more than one psychological type can usually assume the same status personality and perform the roles associated with the status at least adequately (pp. 476–7).

Some theorists distinguish between the *role* (or "status personality") and the *self*, an "'internal organization of qualities (traits, attitudes and habits)" (Sarbin, 1954, p. 224), with "personality" as the inclusive term for both role and self, and for the actions arising from their interplay. For the anthropologist, the role is an "explicit" or readily observable aspect of the individual, while the self is an "implicit" aspect, relatively inaccessible to even the trained observer.

To appreciate how much of an advance this represents over previous sociological understanding of individual behavior, one might take William Graham Sumner (1906) as a reference point. A surprisingly large proportion of sociologists have been content with what are essentially equivalents of this view for an amazingly long time. He glossed over problems of individual variation with dicta to the effect that ". . . all the life of human beings in all ages and stages of culture is primarily controlled by a vast mass of folkways handed down from the earliest existence of the race" (p. 570).

The essence of this simplified social conditioning theory is to reduce all of a man to his overt roles. Its long survival becomes understandable if one looks into its many advantages, for without requiring difficult investigations of individual characteristics or past history, the mere knowledge of his role identity provides a good indication of his social manner, style of life, education, and so forth.

ROLE CONTEXTS: EXPLICIT AND IMPLICIT

In contrast to the personality concept and its concern with the individual person, the idea of role is, then, connected with social contexts or settings. These settings may be seen as a system of cues inviting response, an important component of any such cue being the behavior of others who are a part of the situation. A principle implied here is that one is sustained in his conventional role through the pressure of others as they play out their reciprocal roles. The process is nicely overstated in an ancient and sentimental Hollywood film whose plot concerns a Chicago racketeer who, finding himself heir to an English peerage, moves into the family manor to hide out from enemies. His brutal, bullying approach brings only confused responses from old servants and family retainers who, clutching onto their accustomed ways, insist on seeing him as a noble man. And, gradually, the prevailing deference and trust evoke his reciprocal behavior as a paternalistic, protective gentleman.

Stated less dramatically, a role in a stable system will persist in a relatively unchanging way, despite turnover in the role's incumbents. Thus, the procedure for analyzing any given role involves observing a sample of incumbents in an adequate range of relevant contexts to determine the common requirements for all without regard to individual differences between them. In this fashion, one can learn what responses tend to be manifested by a set of human beings exposed to certain kinds of settings. Inasmuch as all are members of the same species, and of the same culture, considerable similarity in response to similar circumstances might be anticipated. In actual application, this notion is more surprising to psychologists than to sociologists, for the latter group has long relied on that expectation, explicitly or otherwise. Many psychologists, by contrast, tend to expect that behavior will be determined by "personality," seen as an enduring set of individual response tendencies relatively unmodified by specific current contexts.

J. McVicker Hunt makes precisely this point in a stimulating paper written in 1965. There he notes that specialists in personality tend to believe that "the source of most of the variations in behavior resides within persons"—that is, apart from current settings. In an effort to test this assumption, he and two colleagues investigated anxiety responses in samples of freshman and sophomore university students. His findings were interesting, not only in themselves but for their effect on other personologists, who found it difficult to accept that circumstances might predict one's behavior more accurately than one's personality-test scores.

In one sample of Illinois sophomores, with the middle 70 per cent on a measure of anxiousness removed, the mean square for situation (152) was 3.8 times that for persons (40); and in another sample of unselected Penn State freshmen the mean square for situations (244) was somewhat more than 11 times that for persons (21). When we have recited these facts to our colleagues, some of them have criticized our comparing of mean squares. Nevertheless, they have typically paid us the compliment of staring in disbelief (p. 134).

In another context Sargent and Williamson make a very similar observation when they criticize

... the conflicting and not always meaningful lists of traits that emerge from factor analysis of personality questionnaires. Part of the confusion, at least, arises from the fact that data analyzed in such studies are obtained without reference to specific social situations (1966, p. 401).

If this discussion appears to imply that information about "role" and "setting" is sufficient in itself to allow for precise predictions about human behavior, the appearance is deceiving. For all of its appealing advantages, the potentialities of role theory have been impeded by many complexities not immediately apparent. A book-length review of the subject can be found in Biddle (1961), and a more recent critique in Dewey and Humber (1966, especially Chapt. 9). Even apart from such library research, however, the discerning reader might point to Rainwater's 1966 study, reprinted in this volume, to challenge the explanatory utility of the concepts of "role" and "setting." There is little in the explicit roles of lower class husband and wife to clarify Rainwater's assertion that their relationship is emotionally more distant than that of middle class spouses. And yet marital intimacy has been found to be a status-related characteristic (see also Komarovsky, 1962; and Grey, in this collection). For an understanding of the phenomenon, Rainwater turns to implicit features of lower class marital roles such as personality style and interests. The explicit sexual roles for the lower class status level are, if anything, misleading and, much like the symptomatic spots in measles, only superficially associated with key implicit processes.

In his concern with careful and detailed study of the "implicit" features of living at a given social level, Rainwater's study is indicative of an important recent trend in class-character research—a movement away from the reconstruction of psychodynamic "socialization" histories and toward examination of current living conditions. This is seen in the later papers of our collection (Zunich, Miller and Riessman, Pearlin and Kohn, as well as Rainwater). These articles also reflect the fact that research activity has been directed primarily toward the lower class in recent years, testimony to the fact that public concern influences the availability of research funds. There have been a few recent studies of elite groups (see Mills, 1959 and Baltzell, 1958), but unfortunately the rich are not inclined to expose themselves to detailed public scrutiny and are somewhat better able than the poor to control the situation.

Among the best known investigators of the lower class is Oscar Lewis, whose concept of the "culture of poverty" has become quite influential as a result of his persuasive writing. He summarizes his idea in these words (1959):

> Poverty becomes a dynamic factor which affects participation in the larger national culture and creates a subculture of its own. One can speak of the culture of the poor for it has its own modalities and distinctive social and psychological consequences for its members. . . . For example, I am impressed by the remarkable similarities in family structure, the nature of kinship ties, the quality of husband-wife and parent-child relations, time orientation, spending pattern, value systems, and the sense of community found in lower-class settlements in London, in Puerto Rico, in Mexico City slums and Mexican villages and among lower class Negroes in the United States (p. 16).

A contrary view, however, is that due to its extensive mass communications systems the United States is rather homogeneous culturally, and without distinct subcultures—or, at any rate, without subcultural variations influential enough to outweigh individual psychological patterns in accounting for the special characteristics of the extremely poor. A study of the economically deprived in Washington, D.C., has led another Lewis, Hylan Lewis (1967), to these conclusions:

> Our material suggests that neither the quality of life in most low income neighborhoods nor the varying child rearing behaviors of low income families observed by our staff is to be interpreted as generated by, or guided by, "a cultural system in its own right—with an integrity of its own." . . . In fact, many low income families appear here as the frustrated victims of what are thought of as middle class values, behavior, and aspirations (p. 11).

The difference between the two researchers recalls Oscar Lewis' earlier disagreement with Robert Redfield about the characteristics of a Mexican village, but since Lewis has no sharply defined formulation for personality, and has continued to use the impressionistic investigative style characteristic of the older personality-and-culture tradition, the accuracy of his position is again difficult to assess until his sensitive perceptions of the implicit culture and character of the poor are put to systematic test. Partisans of more explicit psychological description may be encouraged, however, by another group of studies.

PERSONALITY THEORY IN A SOCIAL CONTEXT

A great potential strength of role theory, and its advantage over simple social conformity notions (as in Sumner), lies in the fact that it can be integrated with personality concepts to provide explanations for behavior beyond, or counter to, social prescriptions. The matter is illustrated nicely by Inkeles (1959) in a comparison he makes between two approaches to a classic sociological problem. In 1897, Durkheim studied suicide rates quite apart from individual psychological data and discovered certain regularities; these he explained without recourse to personality concepts beyond postulating a human need for a "transcending" loyalty. This work has long stood as a model of sociological analysis. In 1954, however, when Henry and Short analyzed suicide rates, together with homicide, they postulated that both kinds of acts are expressions of aggression in response to frustration. Moreover, they extrapolated from available evidence to propose that characterological orientations at upper social levels lead to internalization of aggressive impulses, but to an opposite expression at lower levels. By this approach they were able "to suggest important connections between suicide and homicide rates, to resolve certain contradictions in Durkheim's analysis, to explain some new data in a manner consistent with the rest of the analysis, and to suggest important lines of further research" (p. 253).

This study also illustrates use of the concept of "modal personality." Similar to Fromm's prior formulation of "social character," Inkeles offers "modal personality" to deal with the problem of the wide variety of personality types to be expected in various subgroups of a complex modern culture. It refers to the particular character patterning most typical for a given social structure and implies that any one formulation should be utilized only insofar as it actually represents the central tendency of a specified group. Thus, research into status and character can be treated as an experiment in nature whereby relations may be traced between specific, empirically established personality tendencies and related social conditions. The first paper in our selection to postulate a modal personality pattern is Schneider and Lysgaard's (1953), but it can be seen that the practice is more frequent in more recent investigations.

Among the significant conditions for any given status is the role behavior expected from those who occupy it. What is the effect on the personality when one is required to enter repeatedly into given social situations and respond to them in the particular ways determined by social pressures? In his 1954 paper on "Role Theory," Sarbin considered this problem and suggested that roles become "internalized," incorporated into the personalities of their actors to varying extents, depending on considerations like characterological predispositions, social desirability of the role, and so forth. This proposition is supported by the results of various experimenters who have required their subjects to express beliefs not part of their original orientations, even antithetical to them (see, for example, Janis and King, 1954; Culbertson, 1957; Scott, 1957; Festinger, 1957). Unfortunately, such studies neglect to investigate relevant implicit processes of the "self" and its influence on internalization.

More dramatic and significant evidence is offered in descriptions by participant observers at concentration camps who saw dramatic changes in the behavior and orientation of inmates. A number of such reports are reviewed by Stanley Elkins in connection with his compelling analysis of the effects of slavery on the American Negro (1959, pp. 103–132). Compensating for the informal nature of their observations is their value as a source of hypotheses. They note a whole constellation of reactions not explainable as simple conformity, and understandable only in psychological terms as dynamic responses of the human organism to certain stresses.

Like the "culture of poverty" studies, they relate behavior to *ongoing* social situations, and, in so doing, break with the older, Freudian emphasis on the processes of development and socialization. It would be misleading, however, to equate psychodynamic thinking with an exclusive emphasis upon childhood training. In fact, the shift in class-culture research has paralleled certain innovations in neo-Freudian theory, including an increased attention to interpersonal transactions in the immediate present (see Horney 1939, and May, 1961). Some social scientists explicitly favor these theories (Elkins, 1959, for example, and Gerth and Mills, 1953), some prefer orthodox psychoanalysis (Kluckhohn, 1954; Parsons, 1958), and some incline to learning theories (Dollard and Miller, 1950; Whiting and Child, 1953). The most significant fact, however, is the growing awareness of the need for integration of psychological and sociological thinking, checked against careful empirical research.

SOME PAPERS ON CLASS AND CHARACTER

Our excursion through the literature of class and character has intended to call attention to its multiplicity of problems and dimensions. No collection of eight papers could hope to encompass all facets of the subject, and so the plan is to begin with one important empirical research project as a reference point and to trace out a series of issues emerging from it. The 1943 study conducted in Chicago by Davis and Havighurst seems especially suitable because of its historic and scientific interest. Reporting that the middle class, both Negro and white, is less "permissive" than the lower in child-rearing practices, their work, published in 1946, thereby raised a whole series of questions, many of which are still alive. Problems that were later to prove bones of contention were not at all apparent in 1946, and it took almost a decade before the research findings of others brought matters to a point where the authors felt impelled to write a follow-up statement. That 1955 paper by Havighurst and Davis—which summarizes their original Chicago study, compares it with the discrepant Boston findings of Sears, Maccoby, and Levin, and poses the problems raised by the divergence of their respective results—is the first in our series here.

Among the questions recognized by the Chicago team were:

1. How does one determine the limits of a social class and the extent to which a sampling from it is representative?
2. To what extent do the characteristics of a given class in the United States vary with geography and ethnic origins?
3. How accurate is the interview, which relies on verbal expression of attitudes, as a means for discovering actual parent-child practices of respondents?

Subsequent research was to turn up other puzzles unanticipated even at this later date. As in an O. Henry story, there came a series of surprise twists, uncovering new questions to replace or compound those not yet solved. When Martha White, for instance, undertook a California investigation to determine whether the Chicago or the Boston report was the more accurate, she concluded that they both were correct! In the article appearing as the second chapter here, she suggested (as did Bronfenbrenner a year later) that they diverged for reasons that had not occurred to Havighurst and Davis—that is, that middle class child-rearing practices were changing so rapidly that what had been true in 1942 no longer held in 1952. Her own data made her fairly confident that ethnic and geographic factors had not been important.

Several issues seemed to have been settled, but the adequacy of a verbal report was still an open question. Several years later (1961), Zunich explored the question of whether attitudes expressed by mothers correspond with observed interaction with their children. His paper, the third chapter in our collection, reports "a lack of statistically significant relationships . . . between maternal attitudes toward children and most of the selected behavior of mothers in an unstructured laboratory setting. . . ." As Zunich explained, these findings might be interpreted in a variety of ways, but they most certainly do not tend to enhance confidence in the verbal report as used in the foregoing investigations. And, insofar as the interview continues to be a major methodological procedure, the problem is still very much alive. One possible solution is to improve the quality of the interview. For instance, clinical observation of total interview interaction can be converted into statistically reliable ratings (see Weinstock, 1967), while another approach is to include direct observation of subjects in real life settings (Grey, 1966). These procedures are costly, however, and for that reason perhaps seldom used. As matters stand, then, many "class-character" studies are more aptly described as "class-verbal expression" research.

Interestingly enough, Zunich's findings do not necessitate rejecting all previous conclusions, for he still found significant differences in *observed* behavior between class levels. These can be seen in his 1961 paper but were pointed out more clearly in a passing reference made in a later article by other writers: "If any conclusion is warranted from the studies which have employed direct observation, it is that the middle class child in contrast to the lower class child lives in a parent dominated world" (J. Walters *et al.*, 1964, p. 440). This would seem to restore the original Davis-Havighurst contention, overthrown by the later Boston study, that middle class parents are less permissive.

Still, in the light of subsequent papers included here, the matter is not nearly so clear as it might seem. Unfortunately, Zunich's methodological rigor was not matched by an equal clarity of conceptualization, a problem that he shares with other investigators. The notions of domination, permissiveness, and so forth, have had general currency in socialization studies but their ambiguities of connotation are seldom eliminated. The Chicago, Boston, and California studies, and those concerned with oral and anal training, were all concerned with these variables that emerged from psychoanalytic thought, but their approach, loose and exploratory, left many discernible loopholes. What does permissiveness include? Is a mother who is active in a "helping" way less permissive than a mother who is "out of contact"? Perhaps she is less responsive rather than more indulgent? Does permissiveness imply indifference? or encouragement? or both? Does it include both the encouragement of autonomy and the encouragement of impulsiveness?

To tighten the conceptualization of personality paradigms in this field, Schneider and Lysgaard published in 1953 a formulation of the "deferred gratification pattern." It is the fourth article reprinted here. They regarded that pattern as a "close approximation" to the notions of Davis and Havighurst and to "bits of research" by others intended to identify a dimension of character differentiating middle class behavior from that of the lower class. The core idea is that the socially higher group tends more toward "renunciation of impulses, making it more capable of carrying out long range programs, like education and saving money, and less inclined toward the emotion-impelled activities like fighting and making love."

From the authors' discussion it is not clear whether this self-discipline is in the service of autonomy or conformity, but the terminology suggests Freud's notion of the "superego" rather than Weber's "Protestant Ethic." For example, speaking of conscience as "instinctual renunciation" (see Freud, 1930, p. 114), Freud relates it to the process of "sublimation by which we subscribe to the general standard which estimates social aims above sexual . . ." (1943, p. 302). The connection is noted as an interesting example of the seepage of the psychoanalytic into the sociological, but, more important, it makes explicit the connotations of the researchers.

By 1961, Miller and Riessman were to protest vigorously that while class-character research had launched Davis and Havighurst's sympathetic portrait of the lower class as warm and free, many papers were now adopting a "pejorative" attitude toward the behavior of the poor as socially undesirable. As the article is included here as the fifth chapter, there is no need to reiterate the exception they take to other views beyond noting a few key issues—their concern over the failure of many writers to identify the central issues and view them accurately, their rejection of both "authoritarianism" and "impulsive gratification" as characterizations of the working-class value orientation, and their suggestion of a third construct, "traditionalism" (which seems quite like "authoritarianism" to this writer, except for its qualities of warmth and family "cooperation").

Perhaps most noteworthy is Miller and Riessman's objection to the "psychologizing" of previous research and their pointing to "cognitive" and "structural" factors as worthy of more attention. Their own focus on structural factors, similar to Kriesberg's later (1963) interest in "circumstances," leads them to discover a significant difference between the "regularly employed" working class (or upper-lowers) and the nonemployed (lower-lower). This calls into question the sampling procedures of all those studies, including several in our own collection, which throw both of these groups into a single "lower class" for comparison with the middle class. The next article, an abridgment of one of my own papers, implicitly contradicts Miller and Riessman in several respects, including the use of the concept of authoritarianism. Essentially, however, it is concerned with a special problem and a special population—the emotionally disturbed, and in that connection it provides an overview of the field together with a more detailed clinical description of a lower class group than is provided elsewhere.

Continuing the comparison of value systems of various social levels, the eighth article reprinted here is Rainwater's 1966 refutation of the core idea of the "deferred gratification pattern." His data indicate that the poor enjoy sex less than do the middle class, pointing a moral for Schneider and Lysgaard who made assertions beyond their findings on this issue. Whereas their work would seem to agree with Miller and Riessman, it actually contradicts their view of the working class home as warm and cooperative, for Rainwater finds traditionalism characterized by emotional separation between husband and wife. His paper seems to suggest that what intrudes on mutual pleasure is the wife's feeling about sex as a "duty," her difficulty in responding with "autonomous interest"—in short, an authoritarian atmosphere.

Our final chapter, a 1966 paper by Pearlin and Kohn, is concerned with two important issues common to these studies and to the literature in general. One of them is the relative authoritarianism of the lower class. Because terms vary and meanings are often obscure, a short summary of the positions of the other articles in our collection on this matter might be helpful. Havighurst and Davis, White, and Zunich, all found the lower class more permissive and so, by implication at least, less authoritarian. Schneider and Lysgaard, in attributing a "deferred gratification pattern" to the middle class, were implying a stricter superego, strong in the sense of social conformity rather than self-determination. Thus, they were essentially agreeing with the previous writers, as was their stated intention. More complex is the position of Miller and Riessman who disagree both with the idea of the lower class as given to impulsive gratification (the less authoritarian position) and with the notion of lower class authoritarianism. Their gentler label for the lower class value system, "traditionalism," indicates that although they do see many authoritarian elements in that subculture, they wish to dissociate themselves from the judgmental overtones of that term. In my paper and in Rainwater's, lower class traditionalism is also discussed, but here the term encompasses qualities additional to the ones in Miller and Riessman. Finally, it should be recalled that however wide the range of behavior discussed, the systematic evidence in most papers is limited to *verbally stated value systems* and does not include all that is implied in the psychodynamic concept of authoritarian character.

At this point "authoritarianism" or, if you prefer, "traditionalism," seems badly in need of further clarification. Pearlin and Kohn provide that in what is, retrospectively, a very simple fashion. They observe that both middle and lower class parents value control, the difference lying in the *source* of control: for the middle class it is internal and for the working class external—self-direction for the one, conformity to proscription for the other. Herein lies "most clearly the essential difference between the middle class emphasis . . . and the working class emphasis," say the authors.

Looking back, one can see that our other writers did not focus on this crucial difference in control and discipline. Possibly this has to do with the source from which they drew their underlying personality conceptions, whether consciously or unconsciously. As Fromm indicates, "Freud's analysis of the superego is the analysis of the authoritarian conscience only" (1947, p. 34). Lacking the distinction between self-direction and external direction, a good case can be made for equal parental emphasis on discipline at either level.

The second issue considered by Pearlin and Kohn is "What precisely is it about class that generates differences in parental values?" Here they are concerned with the problem Kriesberg and Lewis, among others, have raised about the influence of a class culture deriving from socialization over the concrete realities of circumstances, structure, and role demands. In this case, Pearlin and Kohn limit their investigation to the authority structure of the father's occupation, again moving their inquiry to a higher level of specificity than did earlier studies. (Schneider and Lysgaard made a similar attempt but seem to have been less apt in setting up categories.) Still, while the Pearlin-Kohn results fall into a distinct pattern, enhanced by its cross-national consistency, many questions, as the authors themselves point out, are left unanswered. There is, finally, no immediate danger of exhausting the controversies in class-culture research.

CONCLUSION

The past half century has seen a perceptible evolution in the exploration of culture and personality. Fifty years ago, few social scientists were concerned with characterological phenomena, those few neither studying individual behavior systematically nor even separating it conceptually from group processes. Collaboration with psychoanalysts, however, led to more refined hypotheses about personality styles and their connections with particular institutional practices, and, as interest increased, culture-and-personality investigations led to national-character studies and class-character research. Because these disciplines drew upon an ever wider range of social sciences, they yielded important new results in theory, in method, and in practical applications.

Looking first at theory, the early emphasis was on the socialization of the young as the key determinant of adult behavior. More recently, psychologists and sociologists have shifted their attention to the circumstances of adult life as factors affecting character style. Some studies have even reversed the sequence postulated earlier and investigated how the life conditions of the adult, one's occupation, for instance, may affect his child-rearing practices. A judicious view is not that the historical or socialization explanation is irrelevant. Rather, it needs to be complemented by consideration of current situational influences and the relative predictive value of any given approach determined empirically.

To implement such research it has been necessary to devise

new terms for thinking about personality so that individual behavior can be seen more readily in relation to the social environment. Concepts like modal personality and role theory have been advanced to serve this purpose. Alongside these refinements in the personality variable of the personality-culture equation, there also have been clarifications of the second variable, the sociological factors. The description of social systems, particularly status hierarchies, is now much more amenable to mapping and measurement. Thus, far more precisely than several decades ago, a current researcher can locate an individual in his social environment. And he also can depict the individual's responses more readily with reference to particular personality patterns like authoritarianism (despite considerable room for improvement in the formulation of such patterns).

It is in measurement, perhaps, and in the use of systematic research plans, that the field has made some of its most conspicuous strides. At its best, the American academic emphasis on scientific method has demanded rigorous determination of facts to clarify controversial issues. It has mistrusted theoretical rumination backed only by impressionistic evidence. In this respect, class-character research has improved considerably on the earlier work in culture and personality. On the other hand, the newer discipline does not compare so favorably in the generation of fresh ideas. In part this is because careful research is slow work. Translation of concepts into operational terms can be more demanding of intellect and time than the original bright notion which impelled a study. And yet, there is the danger that the methodological concern may degenerate into "scientism" or a concern with the forms of investigation at the expense of significance. Slow progress in class-culture theory may reflect scientistic elements in the role of the social psychologist. Similarly, the current prejudice against considering genetic influences in class-character research (the connection between race and intelligence, for instance) may be related to still other social role influences.

These difficulties have not kept the discipline from making contributions of substantial practical promise. Consider the impact of psychosocial research on the psychoanalytic sources from which it originally drew ideas—an influence important in the development of neo-Freudian innovations in the treatment of emotional disorders. The conceptual fertility of psychodynamics and the methodological sophistication of social science have proven mutually beneficial in combination. Despite its troubles, their marriage is producing healthy offspring. Not the least of them is the series of studies that has evolved into a new approach in the mental health professions. Community psychiatry depends on sociological and psychodynamic insights. The same principles are being extended, too, into the education of the underprivileged and efforts at the reconstruction of their social milieux.

REFERENCES

Adorno, T. W., E. Frenkel-Brunswik, D. J. Levinson, and R. N. Sanford, *The Authoritarian Personality* (New York: Harper & Row, 1950).

Alpert, H., "Sociology: Its Present Interests," in B. Berelson, ed., *The Behavioral Sciences Today* (New York: Harper & Row [Harper Torchbooks], 1964).

Anderson, H. E., *The Young Child in the Home* (New York: Appleton-Century-Crofts, 1936).

Aristotle, "Social Classes: A Classical View," in R. Bendix and S. M. Lipset, eds., *Class, Status and Power* (New York: The Free Press, 1953).

Baltzell, E. D., *Philadelphia Gentlemen* (New York: The Free Press, 1958).

Bateson, G., *Naven* (Cambridge, England: Cambridge University Press, 1936).

Bell, D., "Modernity and Mass Society: On the Varieties of Cultural Experience," *Studies in Public Communication*, 4 (1962).

Benedict, R., *Patterns of Culture* (Boston: Houghton Mifflin, 1934).

Biddle, B. J., *The Present Status of Role Theory* (Columbia: University of Missouri Press, 1961).

Bronfenbrenner, U., "Socialization and Social Class through Time and Space," in E. E. Maccoby, T. M. Newcomb, and E. L. Hartley, eds., *Readings in Social Psychology* (New York: Holt, Rinehart & Winston, 1958).

Broom, L., "Social Differentiation and Stratification," in R. K. Merton, L. Broom, and L. S. Cottrell, Jr., eds., *Sociology Today* (New York: Basic Books, 1959), pp. 429–41.

Brown, R., *Social Psychology* (New York: The Free Press, 1965).

44 : *Introduction*

Centers, R., *The Psychology of Social Classes* (Princeton: Princeton University Press, 1949).

Chapin, F. S., "A Quantitative Scale for Rating the Home and Social Environment of Middle-Class Families in an Urban Community," *Journal of Educational Psychology*, 19 (1928).

Child, I. L., "Socialization," in G. Lindzey, ed., *Handbook of Social Psychology* (2 vols., Reading, Mass.: Addison-Wesley, 1954).

Christie, R., and M. Jahoda, eds., *Studies in the Scope and Method of "The Authoritarian Personality"* (New York: The Free Press, 1954).

Culbertson, F. M., "Modification of an Emotionally Held Attitude through Role Playing," *Journal of Abnormal and Social Psychology*, 54 (1957), 230–33.

Davis, A., *Social-Class Influences upon Learning* (Cambridge: Harvard University Press, 1949).

Davis, A., and J. Dollard, *Children of Bondage* (Washington, D.C.: American Council on Education, 1940).

Davis, A., B. B. Gardner, and M. R. Gardner, *Deep South* (Chicago: University of Chicago, 1941).

Davis, A., and R. J. Havighurst, *Father of the Man: How Your Child Gets His Personality* (Boston: Houghton Mifflin, 1947).

Davis, A., and R. J. Havighurst, "Social Class and Color Differences in Child-Rearing," *American Sociological Review*, 11 (1946), 697–710.

Dewey, R., and W. J. Humber, *An Introduction to Social Psychology* (New York: Macmillan, 1966).

Dollard, J., *Caste and Class in a Southern Town* (New Haven: Yale University Press, 1937).

Dollard, J., *Criteria for the Life History* (New Haven: Yale University Press, 1935).

Dollard, J., L. W. Doob, N. E. Miller, and R. R. Sears, *Frustration and Aggression* (New Haven: Yale University Press, 1939).

Dollard, J., and N. E. Miller, *Personality and Psychotherapy: An Analysis in Terms of Learning, Thinking, and Culture* (New York: McGraw-Hill, 1950).

DuBois, C., *The People of Alor: A Social-Psychological Study of an East Indian Island* (Minneapolis: University of Minnesota Press, 1944).

Duijker, H. C. J., and N. H. Frijda, *National Character and National Stereotypes: A Trend Report Prepared for the International Union of Scientific Psychology* (Amsterdam: North Holland Publishing Co., 1960).

Durkheim, E., *Suicide* (New York: The Free Press, 1951).

Elkins, S., *Slavery* (Chicago: University of Chicago Press, 1959).

Ericson, M., "Child-Rearing and Social Status," *American Journal of Sociology*, 53 (1946), 190–92.

Fenichel, O., *The Psychoanalytic Theory of Neuroses* (New York: W. W. Norton, 1945).

Festinger, L., *A Theory of Cognitive Dissonance* (New York: Harper & Row, 1957).

Frank, L. K., *Society as the Patient* (New Brunswick: Rutgers University Press, 1948).

ALAN L. GREY : 45

Freud, S., *Civilization and Its Discontents* (London and New York: The Hogarth Press, 1930).

Freud, S., *A General Introduction to Psychoanalysis* (New York: Garden City Publishing, 1943).

Fromm, E., *Escape from Freedom* (New York: Holt, Rinehart & Winston, 1941).

Gerth, H., and C. W. Mills, *Character and Social Structure* (New York: Harcourt, Brace & World, 1953).

Gorer, G., *The American People: A Study in National Character* (New York: W. W. Norton, 1948).

Grey, A., "Social Class and the Psychiatric Patient: A Study in Composite Character," *Contemporary Psychoanalysis*, 2 (1966), 87–121.

Grey, A., "Relationships between Social Status and Psychological Characteristics of Psychiatric Patients" (unpublished doctoral dissertation; Chicago: University of Chicago, 1949).

Havighurst, R., and A. Davis, "A Comparison of the Chicago and Harvard Studies of Social-Class Differences in Child Rearing," *American Sociological Review*, 20 (1955), 438–41.

Henry, A. F., and J. F. Short, *Suicide and Homicide* (New York: The Free Press, 1954).

Hodges, H. M., Jr., *Social Stratification* (Cambridge, Mass.: Schenkman, 1964).

Hollingshead, A. B., *Elmtown's Youth* (New York: John Wiley, 1949).

Hollingshead, A. B., and F. Redlich, *Social Class and Mental Illness* (New York: Wiley, 1958).

Horney, K., *New Ways in Psychoanalysis* (London: Routledge and Kegan Paul, 1939).

Hunt, J. McV., "Traditional Personality Theory in the Light of Recent Evidence," *American Scientist*, 53 (1965), 80–96.

Inkeles, A., "Personality and Social Structure," in R. K. Merton, L. Broom, and L. S. Cottrell, Jr., eds., *Sociology Today: Problems and Prospects* (New York: Basic Books, 1959), pp. 249–76.

Inkeles, A., "Some Sociological Observations on Culture and Personality Studies," in C. Kluckhohn, H. A. Murray, and D. M. Schneider, eds., *Personality in Nature, Society, and Culture* (second edition; New York: A. Knopf, 1953), pp. 577–92.

Inkeles, A., and D. J. Levinson, "National Character: The Study of Modal Personality and Sociocultural Systems," in G. Lindzey, ed., *Handbook of Social Psychology* (2 vols.; Reading, Mass.: Addison-Wesley, 1954).

Janis, I. L., C. I. Hovland, P. B. Field, H. Linton, E. Graham, A. R. Cohen, D. Rife, R. P. Abelson, G. S. Lesser, and B. T. King, *Personality and Persuasibility* (New Haven: Yale University Press, 1959).

Janis, I. L., and B. T. King, "The Influence of Roleplaying on Opinion-Change, *Journal of Abnormal and Social Psychology*, 49 (1954), 211–18.

Kahl, J. A., and J. A. Davis, "A Comparison of Indexes of Socio-Economic Status," *American Sociological Review*, 20 (1955), 317–25.

Kardiner, A., *The Individual and His Society* (New York: Columbia University Press, 1939).

Kardiner, A., *et al.*, *The Psychological Frontiers of Society* (New York: Columbia University Press, 1945).

Kardiner, A., and E. Preble, *They Studied Man* (New York: New American Library [Mentor Books], 1963).

Kluckhohn, C., "Culture and Behavior," in G. Lindzey, ed., *Handbook of Social Psychology* (Cambridge: Mass.: Addison-Wesley, 1954).

Kluckhohn, C., H. A. Murray, and D. M. Schneider, eds., *Personality in Nature, Society, and Culture* (second edition; New York: A. Knopf, 1953).

Kluckhohn, C., "Some Aspects of Navaho Infancy and Early Childhood," in G. Roheim, ed., *Psychoanalysis and the Social Sciences* (vol. 1; New York: International Universities Press, 1947).

Kohn, M. L., "Social Class and Parent-Child Relationships: An Interpretation," in F. Riessman, J. Cohen, and A. Pearl, eds., *Mental Health of the Poor: New Treatment Approaches for Low Income People* (New York: The Free Press, 1964).

Komarovsky, M., *Blue-Collar Marriage* (New York: Random House, 1962).

Kornhauser, W. R., "The Warner Approach to Social Stratification," in R. Bendix and S. M. Lipset, eds., *Class, Status, and Power: A Reader in Social Stratification* (New York: The Free Press, 1953).

Kriesberg, L., "The Relationship between Socio-Economic Rank and Behavior," *Social Problems*, 16 (1963), 334–53.

Lewis, H., *Culture, Class and Poverty* (Washington, D.C.: Cross-Tell, 1967).

Lewis, O., *Five Families* (New York: Basic Books, 1959).

Lewis, O., *Life in a Mexican Village: Tepoztlán Restudied* (Urbana: University of Illinois Press, 1951).

Lindzey, G., *Projective Techniques and Cross-Cultural Research* (New York: Appleton-Century-Crofts, 1961).

Linton, R., *The Cultural Background of Personality* (London: Routledge & Kegan Paul, 1952).

MacIver, R. M., *Society: Its Structure and Changes* (New York: Long and Smith, 1931).

MacKinnon, D. W., "The Structure of Personality," in J. McV. Hunt, ed., *Personality and the Behavior Disorders* (2 vols.; New York: Ronald, 1944).

Malinowski, B., *Sex and Repression in Savage Society* (London: Humanities Press, 1927).

Marx, K., *Capital, the Communist Manifesto and Other Outings: Edited with an Introduction by Max Eastman, with an Unpublished Essay on Marxism by Lenin* (New York: Modern Library, 1932).

May, R., ed., *Existential Psychology* (New York: Random House, 1961).

Mead, M., *From the South Seas: Studies of Adolescence and Sex in Primitive Societies* (New York: William Morrow, 1939).

Miller, S. M., and F. Riessman, "The Working Class Subculture: A New View," *Social Problems*, 9 (1961), 86–97.

Mills, C. W., *The Power Elite* (New York: Oxford University Press [Galaxy Books], 1959).

Minturn, L., and W. W. Lambert, *Mothers of Six Cultures: Antecedents of Child Rearing* (New York: John Wiley, 1964).

North, C. C., and P. K. Hatt, "Jobs and Occupations: A Popular Evaluation," *Public Opinion News*, 9 (1947), 3–13.

Page, C. H., *Class and American Sociology: From Ward to Ross* (New York: Dial Press, 1940).

Parsons, T., "Social Structure and the Development of Personality—Freud's Contribution to the Integration of Psychology and Sociology," *Psychiatry*, 21 (1958), 321–40.

Parsons, T., "A Revised Analytical Approach to the Theory of Social Stratification," in R. Bendix and S. M. Lipset, eds., *Class, Status and Power* (New York: The Free Press, 1953).

Parsons, T., and E. A. Shils, *Toward a General Theory of Action: Theoretical Foundations for the Social Sciences* (Cambridge, Mass.: Harvard University Press, 1951).

Pearlin, L. I., and M. L. Kohn, "Social Class Occupation and Parental Values: A Cross-National Study," *American Sociological Review*, 31 (1966), 466–79.

Pitts, J. R., "Introduction: Personality and the Social System," in T. Parsons, E. A. Shils, K. D. Naegele, and J. R. Pitts, eds., *Theories of Society: Foundations of Modern Sociological Theory* (New York: The Free Press, 1961), pp. 683–716.

Rainwater, L., "Some Aspects of Lower Class Sexual Behavior," *Journal of Social Issues*, 22 (1966), 96–107.

Redfield, R. *Tepoztlán, a Mexican Village: A Study of Folk Life* (Chicago: University of Chicago Press, 1946).

Riessman, F., J. Cohen, and A. Pearl, *Mental Health of the Poor* (New York: The Free Press, 1964).

Samelson, F., and J. F. Yates, "Acquiescence and the F Scale: Old Assumptions and the New Data, *Psychological Bulletin*, 68 (1967), 91-103.

Sapir, E., "Culture, Genuine and Spurious," *American Journal of Sociology*, 29 (1924), 401-28.

Sarbin, T. R., "Role Theory," in G. Lindzey, ed., *Handbook of Social Psychology* (Reading, Mass: Addison-Wesley, 1954), pp. 223-58.

Sargent, S. S., and R. C. Williamson, *Social Psychology* (third edition; New York: Ronald Press, 1966).

Schaar, J. H., *Escape from Authority: The Perspectives of Erich Fromm* (New York: Basic Books, 1961).

Schneider, L., and S. Lysgaard, "The Deferred Gratification Pattern: A Preliminary Study," *American Sociological Review*, 18 (1953), 142–49.

Scott, W. A., "Attitude Change through Reward of Verbal Behavior," *Journal of Abnormal and Social Psychology*, 55 (1957), 72–75.

Sorokin, P., *Contemporary Sociological Theories* (New York: Harper & Row, 1928).

Sullivan, H. S., *Conceptions of Modern Psychiatry* (Washington, D.C.: William Alanson White Psychiatric Foundation, 1947).

Sumner, W. G., *Folkways* (Boston: Ginn, 1906).

Thompson, C., *Psychoanalysis: Evolution and Development* (New York: Thomas Nelson and Sons, 1950).

Walters, J., R. Connor, and M. Zunich, "Interaction of Mothers and Children from Lower-Class Families," *Child Development*, 35 (1964), 433–40.

Warner, W. L., R. L. Havighurst, and M. Loeb, *Who Shall Be Educated?* (New York: Harper & Row, 1944).

Warner, W. L., and J. O. Low, *The Social System of the Modern Factory* (New Haven: Yale University Press, 1947).

Warner, W. L., and P. S. Lunt, *The Status System of a Modern Community* (New Haven: Yale University Press, 1942).

Warner, W. L., and P. S. Lunt, *The Social Life of a Modern Community* (New Haven: Yale University Press, 1941).

Warner, W. L., M. Meeker, and K. Eells, *Social Class in America: The Evaluation of Status* (Chicago: Science Research Associates, 1949).

Warner, W. L., and L. Srole, *The Social System of America's Ethnic Groups* (New Haven: Yale University Press, 1945).

Weber, M., *The Theory of Social and Economic Organization,* trans. A. M. Henderson and Talcott Parsons, ed. Talcott Parsons (New York: The Free Press, 1947).

Weinstock, A. R., "Family Environment and the Development of Defense and Coping Mechanisms," *Journal of Personality and Social Psychology,* 5 (1967), 67–75.

White, M. S., "Social Class, Child Rearing Practices and Child Behavior," *American Sociological Review,* 22 (1957), 704–12.

Whiting, B., ed., *Six Cultures: Studies of Child Rearing* (New York: John Wiley, 1963).

Whiting, J. W. M., and I. L. Child, *Child Training and Personality: A Cross-Cultural Study* (New Haven: Yale University Press, 1953).

Zunich, M., "A Study of Relationships between Child Rearing Attitudes and Maternal Behavior," *Journal of Experimental Education,* 30 (1961), 231–41.

1: *A Comparison of the Chicago and Harvard Studies of Social Class Differences in Child Rearing*

ROBERT J. HAVIGHURST

ALLISON DAVIS

In 1951–52 Sears and his colleagues[1] made a study of social class and child-rearing practices which is to some extent comparable with a study made in 1943 by Davis and Havighurst.[2] The results of the two studies agree in some respects and disagree in others. Consequently, it seems useful to present such results of the two studies as are comparable, so as to permit readers to make their own comparisons and draw their own conclusions.

THE SAMPLES

The Harvard interviews were held with mothers of kindergarten children and dealt with the training of the kindergarten child

Reprinted by permission of the authors and publisher from *American Sociological Review*, 20 (August 1955), 438–42. The tables accompanying the original article do not appear here; interested readers are referred to the issue of *ASR* noted above.

only. The Chicago interviews were held with mothers of pre-school age children but dealt with every child of the mother. The Chicago study dealt with the 107 middle and 167 lower class white children of 48 middle and 52 lower class white mothers. The Harvard study, on the other hand, dealt with 201 middle class and 178 lower class white mothers, and with the same numbers of children. The interviewers were college-educated women who were specifically trained to conduct interviews with the particular instrument used in each study.

In order to make the data more nearly comparable, the Chicago data which involved all the children of a mother have been restudied by taking the one child nearest the age of five. This makes the Chicago medians somewhat different, but not greatly so, from those that appear in the original article. Also, to make the data more comparable the Harvard data on the age of beginning and completing weaning and toilet training have been reworked to show medians rather than means.

As would be expected, the nationality backgrounds of the two samples are different. Both had heaviest representation from American, British, or Canadian backgrounds, but in the Boston sample more came from Italian, Spanish, and Greek backgrounds; and in the Chicago sample, more from German, Dutch, Scandinavian and Mexican backgrounds. Nationality was defined as the country of birth of the mother's parents. If one parent was foreign-born, the mother was assigned to a foreign nationality. The occupational status of the fathers in the two samples, based on the Warner scale of occupations, indicates that the Boston sample of lower status parents averages somewhat higher in status than the Chicago sample, due to the inclusion in the Boston lower status sample of a number of lower middle people.

Only 27 per cent of the Boston lower status sample are in the bottom two occupational rankings, while 47 per cent of the Chicago sample are at these two lowest levels. Therefore, the two lower status samples are not easily comparable. However, the report of the Boston study indicates that there was little difference between the upper and lower halves of the lower status sample in child rearing behavior, and the same kinds of differences between the Chicago and Boston studies would have been found if the Boston lower status sample had been restricted to the lowest occupational levels.

The Boston sample was made up of families having a child in kindergarten in the public schools of two sections of the Greater Boston metropolitan area. Interviews were actually obtained with 80 per cent of the mothers of kindergarten children in these particular schools. The Chicago sample of middle class mothers came from two nursery schools on the South Side of Chicago and from a middle class apartment area on the North Side. The Chicago lower class mothers came from three areas on the South Side of Chicago, and most of them did not have children in nursery schools. Interviews were secured with them by passing from one family to another in areas of poor housing. Clearly the Chicago sample is far from a random sample. It was aimed primarily at studying individual differences in personality among children in a family and relating them to the children's experience in the family; and for this purpose it did not seem necessary to have representative social class samples. The social class comparisons were initially thought of as a by-product of the study. The Boston sample would seem in some respects to be more representative, although its being limited to mothers of children in public schools caused the exclusion of Catholic mothers who send their children to parochial schools. The Chicago sample had a number of such Catholic mothers, as well as a few upper middle class mothers whose children were in a private school.

COMPARISONS

Feeding and Weaning

The comparisons on feeding and weaning appear to indicate the following: (1) a regional difference in the amount of breast feeding; (2) a tendency for more breast feeding by lower class

Chicago mothers than by either group of Boston mothers; (3) middle class Chicago mothers completed weaning their children earlier than middle class Boston mothers; (4) a strong tendency for lower class Chicago mothers to use more of a self-demand schedule in feeding than was used by either Boston group. It is in the area of feeding and weaning that the two studies differ most.

Toilet Training

Chicago middle class mothers began bowel training earlier than lower class mothers, while there was no class difference among Boston mothers in this respect. On the other hand, Boston lower class mothers reported completion of bowel training at an earlier age than middle class mothers, while there was no class difference among Chicago mothers. In both studies lower class mothers were reported to be more severe in punishment in relation to toilet training.

Restrictions on Movements of Children Outside of Home

The Chicago mothers reported as follows: Age at which boys and girls might go to the movies alone—lower class reliably earlier; time at which boys and girls are expected in at night—middle class reliably earlier; age at which boys and girls go downtown alone—middle class reliably earlier.

The only Harvard data which are comparable indicate a tendency (not quite significant) for middle class children to be allowed to go farther away from the house during the day. This is probably in agreement with the Chicago finding of age at which children were allowed to go downtown alone.

Expectations for Child to Help in Home

The comparative data on what is expected of children in helping at home indicates that none of the Boston class differences is reliable; the Chicago data indicate a tendency for middle class mothers to expect children to be helpful earlier than lower class mothers do.

Parent-child Relations

There were a number of possible comparisons of parent-child relations, which will be summarized briefly. The amount of care-taking of children by fathers shows no class difference in either study. But when the nature of affectional relationships between father and children is evaluated, the lower class father is found to be reliably less affectionate in the Boston study, while in the Chicago study the lower class father "plays with" his children more, but the middle class father teaches and reads to his children more. The studies are somewhat comparable on the matter of the display of aggression in the home (excluding aggression toward siblings). There are no reliable class differences in either study in this respect.

SUMMARY OF AGREEMENTS BETWEEN THE STUDIES

It will be seen that there are both agreements and disagreements between the results of the Chicago and Boston studies. The principal agreements between the two studies are the following: Lower class is more severe in punishment in toilet-training; middle class has higher educational expectations of their children; no class difference in amount of care given children by father; no class difference in display of aggression by children in the home, excluding aggression toward siblings (data not shown here, but available to the authors); middle class children allowed more freedom of movement away from home during the day.

DISCUSSION OF DISAGREEMENTS BETWEEN THE STUDIES

In discussing the disagreements between the two studies it seems important to determine to what extent the Boston study is a replication of the Chicago study. The interviewing methods used were rather similar, and some nearly identical questions were asked. However, the two samples are not strictly comparable. As we learn more about social structure in the United States, it becomes clear that one should not attempt to generalize concerning child-rearing to an entire social class from a sample in one part of the country, even if it is a representative sample. There may be cultural differences between two samples of apparently similar occupational status, due to regional differences, religious differences, and differences of nationality background, all of which may have been operating in the studies being considered here. Furthermore, there may be differences between different occupational groups within the same social class.[3]

Of considerable importance is the limitation imposed by the method of securing data. To an unknown extent, mothers give what they regard as the "expected" or "appropriate" answers when telling how they raise their children. For instance, the data indicate that the Boston lower class mothers report themselves as less permissive of aggression by their children toward other children in the neighborhood. But this is difficult to fit with the fact that lower class children fight more than middle class children do—a fact on which observers of the social behavior of children agree. Perhaps the fact that mothers were talking about young children (five-year-olds) was significant here; or perhaps the greater frequency of fighting by lower class children actually brings out more of a feeling on the part of their mothers that they should restrain their children's aggression.

It is conceivable, for instance, that middle class mothers are defensive about their *severity* and therefore claim to be less punitive or threatening than in practice they are observed to be; whereas lower class mothers are defensive about their children being *dirty* and *violent* and therefore claim to be more punitive with regard to their children's soiling and fighting than such parents are observed to be. At any rate, this reinforces the conviction of the present writers that the interview is not nearly so good as participant observation for securing data both on the behavior and the attitudes of parents toward their children.

The disagreements between the findings of the two studies are substantial and important. The interviewing seems to have been competent in both studies. Inadequacies of sampling in both studies may be a source of at least some of the differences. Changes in child rearing ideology between 1943 and 1952 may be in some measure responsible for the differences. The problem of interpreting the statements of mothers answering identical questions about their children who are exposed to quite different environmental stimulation is a major one.

REFERENCES

1. Robert R. Sears, Eleanor E. Maccoby and Harry Levin, *Patterns of Child Rearing* (New York: Harper & Row, 1957). See also Eleanor E. Maccoby and Patricia K. Gibbs and the Staff of the Laboratory of Human Development, Harvard University, "Methods of Child Rearing in Two Social Classes," in William E. Martin and Celia Burns Stendler, *Readings in Child Development* (New York: Harcourt, Brace, 1954).

   We wish to thank Robert R. Sears and John W. M. Whiting and particularly Eleanor E. Maccoby for their courtesy in sharing their data with us. One of us visited the Harvard group and compared notes with them, after which Dr. Maccoby supplied us with such data from the Harvard Study as were needed for comparative purposes and advised us on the format of the tables.

2. A. Davis and R. J. Havighurst, "Social Class and Color Differences in Child-Rearing," *American Sociological Review*, 11 (1946), 698–710.

3. Daniel Miller and Guy E. Swanson of the University of Michigan have reported finding differences in child rearing practices between two occupational groups at the same social class level, one group working in a bureaucratic situation with a maximum of order, structure, and routine in their work, while the other group worked in a changing, competitive industry with a premium on initiative, flexibility and mobility in their work.

2: Social Class, Child Rearing Practices, and Child Behavior

MARTHA STURM WHITE

Several recent studies have raised interesting questions about the relation of social class position to child rearing practices. In particular there have been some challenges to the study reported on by Ericson and by Davis and Havighurst.[1] This study, carried out in Chicago in the early 1940's, found the middle class to be generally more severe in weaning and toilet training, and to restrict and put more demands upon the child. Later studies[2] have found several differences, primarily in the direction of more permissiveness by middle class mothers than the Chicago study described.

Reprinted by permission of the author and publisher from *American Sociological Review,* 22 (1957), 704–12.

  Some of the tables in the original article do not appear here; interested readers are referred to the issue of *ASR* noted above.

  This investigation was supported by research grants, MH 208 (C2) and M-836 (MH 1) from the National Institute of Mental Health of the National Institutes of Health, Public Health Service. The data were gathered under the direction of Frances Orr at Stanford University. The author was principal investigator for the latter grant.

What are the causes of these differences? Are the samples not comparable? Are there regional differences? Or have mothers in different social class positions changed their child rearing practices during the intervening decade? The study reported here pertains to these questions. During the first half of 1953, a group of mothers and their children were interviewed on two occasions in a study on the effects of sibling birth. An approximately equal number of middle and working class families were included, so that it was possible to test several social class hypotheses.

The two hypotheses reported on in this article are: (1) child rearing practices have changed since the earlier studies were made; (2) these changes are a result of the different reference groups used by the middle and working class mothers.

Comments on the changing fashions in child rearing are common in popular literature, particularly comments on the increase in permissiveness, and it is possible that these remarks are a reflection of changes in practice. It is, of course, difficult to demonstrate a change when knowledge of prior conditions is scanty. Davis and Havighurst, for example, stress the fact that theirs is not a representative sample. However, it has frequently been taken as representative of child training practices of the time,[3] and since we have no contrary knowledge, it will be accepted as such here. The method of testing is to compare the child training practices found in California in 1953 with those of Chicago in 1943 and of Boston in 1951–52.

How or why changes take place is another question. One possibility, tested here, is that the middle class is most responsive to new ideas in the environment, particularly those transmitted by experts and through mass media. To use Riesman's term, they are "other directed"; that is, they tend to rely on other people (outside of the family) in their environment, and on certain kinds of authority figures.[4] Although both classes rely on mass media, the middle class is more discriminating.

Other studies have established that expert ideas on child rearing have changed from decade to decade.[5] It seems conceivable that if middle class parents are responsive to certain sources of opinion, such as experts and other people, they also might be more apt to change their practices. On this basis, we would expect the middle class to have changed their practices since the 1943 study.

METHOD

The Sample

The sample consisted of 74 mothers and 74 children. All of the mothers had only one child, and the child was between two and one-half and five and one-half years of age. These ages were chosen so that the children would be able to talk, and would be mainly under the influence of the family rather than the school. Additional requirements were that the parents be living together and be native born.

The data were gathered during the first half of 1953 in California in the South San Francisco Peninsula area, which does not include San Francisco itself, but a string of suburban and industrial communities stretching from San Mateo to San Jose. Approximately 15 families each came from Palo Alto, Menlo Park, and San Jose, and the remainder from adjacent towns. Although the study was conducted from Stanford University, only a few families had any connection with the university.

The larger study on stress caused by the arrival of a second child in the family,[6] of which this study was a part, required 50 of the mothers to be expecting a second child at the time of the first interview, and the remaining 24 control families (who were not expecting a baby) to be matched on a group basis by occupation of father, neighborhood, age and sex of child. Due to the difficulties of getting such a sample that could also be interviewed over a six month interval, referrals were secured in a variety of ways. They came from neighbors or friends of families already in the study, from Public Health Nurses, personnel managers in industry, from maternal pre-natal exercise classes, from physicians and nursery school teachers, and from school district surveys. Only 14 women, less than 6 per cent of the total 245 contacted, were uninterested or unwilling to be interviewed. The remainder of those not used proved to be ineligible or had moved.

The Interview

The interviewing was done in the home by two experienced psychologists. While one talked to the mother for a period of between one and one-half and three hours, the other "interviewed" the child in his room or in the kitchen by means of doll play, Draw-A-Man tests, and other standard situations. Standard questions were used in the mother interview with follow-up probes. Many of the questions asked were identical with those of the Boston study.[7] The replies of the mother were taken down as nearly verbatim as possible.

THE MEASURES

Social Class

The occupation of the father in the family was rated on a Warner scale with an inter-rater reliability coefficient of .93.[8] A comparison of the occupation status of the two groups may be seen in Table 1. Groups were designated as middle or working class on the basis of an index of occupation and income. Occupation was given a weight of two, income one. The resulting distribution was divided into nine socioeconomic status levels; from 1 to 4 was designated middle class and from 5 to 9, working class. Thus, 36 of the families were classified as middle class, 38 as working class.

This system of class placement has the advantage of making the data comparable to the Boston study and seems a fair approximation to the Chicago data. It also rather accurately divides the group into white-collar and blue-collar occupations. Such a gross, dichotomous classification was used tentatively, but it

TABLE 1: *Socioeconomic Characteristics of the Sample*

	Middle Class	Working Class
Father's occupation (Warner)		
1	15 (42%)	0
2	14 (39%)	1 (3%)
3	7 (19%)	4 (10%)
4	0	10 (26%)
5	0	17 (45%)
6 & 7	0	6 (16%)
Father's education		
Grade school	0	3
7–12 grades	2	19
Some college	34	16
Mother's education		
Grade school	0	1
7–12 grades	7	26
College or technical training	29	11
Occupation of father's father		
Middle (1–3)	26	4
Working (4–7)	10	34
Occupation of mother's father		
Middle (1–3)	22	13
Working (4–7)	14	25
Social class by self-placement		
Middle	32	13
Intermediate	1	4
Working	3	20
"None"		1
Salary		
$5000 or over	32	11
Under $5000	4	27
Age of mother		
28 or under	14	21
Over 28	22	17

proved to be meaningful, not unduly distorting the underlying structure, and seemed appropriate to the size of the sample and the statistical measures used.

Mother-Behavior Variables

The answers to the interview questions were coded, using when possible the same codes as the Boston study. Reliabilities were computed on all, and only those items on which satisfactory reliabilities (.72 or above) were found were used. No reliability rating was possible for personality ratings of mother and child since only one person conducted each interview; consequently these ratings were used as a supplement to the parent behavior data.

Statistical Analysis

Although other investigators have used the t-test for comparison, preliminary study indicated that the variances were not homogeneous on several items, so that chi-square seemed more appropriate for these data. Four-fold tables were used and comparisons made of the number of middle and working class families above and below the median of the variable in question. The break was made at the point that most nearly divided the total group evenly. In some cases a "yes" or "no" classification was more appropriate than the median. In other cases the meaning of the scale was better served by a three-fold classification— the highs, the moderates, and the lows. In these cases such a comparison was first made. This often resulted in low-cell frequencies, and the median comparison was substituted when it did no violence to the relationship as indicated by the three-fold break. The two-tailed test was used and a correction for continuity was employed, since many authorities consider it mandatory for four-fold tables, regardless of cell frequencies.[9]

RESULTS

The comparison of middle and working class on oral behavior and feeding regimen indicates that on the whole there are few social class differences. There are no significant differences in use of breast feeding, duration of breast feeding, age when weaning is completed, extent to which demand feeding is practiced, or severity of feeding problems. There is a very slight tendency for middle class children to have been weaned either younger or older than lower class children (but no difference in average

age of weaning), and for middle class infant oral regimen (an over-all measure scored by a rater) to have been less severe. As in the Chicago and Boston studies, middle class mothers report significantly more thumb sucking. However, working class mothers report significantly more nailbiting, or biting and chewing activity.

In toilet training, no difference was found in age at which bowel training was begun, but working class mothers were significantly more severe in toilet training.

There were no significant differences in dependency—how much the child wanted to be near the mother, wanted attention, objected to separation, or was judged dependent.

When we asked the mothers about obedience training, one rather interesting significant difference was found. If the child did not do what was asked, middle class mothers were significantly more inclined to drop the subject occasionally. However, there was no difference when they were asked if they expected immediate obedience. More mothers in both groups say the father is more strict than they, but there is no class difference.

In an area that might be described as the mother's responsiveness to the child, there was one significant difference—middle class mothers were more responsive to their baby's crying. They did not differ in amount of fun taking care of the baby, in the amount of demonstrativeness shown, or in how much they kept track of the child.

Several of the questions were directed at the topic of aggression. The data show that there were no differences in parents' report of amount of aggression in the home, in their demands for aggression against other children, or in how much the child was encouraged to fight back. One highly significant difference was in permissiveness toward aggression against parents. Middle class women were consistently above the median in feeling that expression of aggression should be allowed. There are some tendencies for the working class children to be more severely punished for aggression against the parent, and to be reported as fighting more with other children.

Did these differences in training methods result in any differences among the children? Practically no class differences were found in tests (such as ability to delay gratification, Draw-A-Man), personality ratings, or aggression in doll play.[10]

Although there was no class difference on source of ideas about child rearing, the most frequently named source was the mother herself—her own ideas, her common sense, her trial and error. There was no class difference between mothers mentioning reading newspapers or magazines, but there was a significant difference if they mentioned a specific book by an expert (Spock or Gesell, for example) rather than newspaper or magazine articles. Middle class mothers mention the expert books more. They also mentioned other people or friends significantly more often as a source of ideas. There were slightly more middle class women who got ideas from child-rearing authorities, such as doctors or nursery instructors, and from parent education classes with other mothers. Although similar numbers of working and middle class mothers mention their own childhoods as sources of ideas, middle class mothers more often mention practices used by their parents which they would modify or reject. Many more sources of ideas were mentioned by the middle class mothers.

A number of questions in the interview were designed to extract explanatory concepts as indicators of the mothers' frames of reference, goals, and personalities. They will not be developed in this paper, but some of the raw class differences are of interest.

When mothers were asked what kind of person they wanted their child to be, they tended to answer in terms of five general categories—they wanted him to be happy, well adjusted, a nice or good person, independent, or liked. There were class differences on two of these. More middle class mothers said "well adjusted," and more working class mothers said "a nice or good child." There were no differences in the degree to which the mothers saw themselves as similar to others in strictness, whether they perceived themselves as similar to their own parents in strictness or in sympathetic understanding, the aspects of parenthood they found most and least enjoyable, or in their own self-descriptions, except that working class women more often spontaneously mentioned that they were neat.

The mothers were also rated by the interviewer on a number of personality variables. Middle class mothers were significantly more secure, independent, and dominant. There was a tendency for them to be more controlled, but no differences in ratings of potential anxiety, hostility, ability to express affect, aggression, constriction, ability to accept dependency, or ability to accept aggression.

DISCUSSION

These results may be compared to those found in Chicago and in Boston (see Table 2). The main topics which all three studies had in common are feeding and toilet training.

In general the results are more in accord with those obtained in 1951–52 in Boston than with those of 1943 in Chicago. Of five variables on which the Chicago study found class differences, we found no difference. Of fourteen variables also used in the Boston study, we found essentially the same results on eleven, and slightly different results on three. Considering the smaller sample size, and the conservatism of the statistical test, this is remarkable agreement. In addition, the over-all picture of the middle class as more permissive and less demanding of the child is in general agreement with the Boston study rather than with the Chicago data.

The relevant question is, of course, whether these differences indicate changes in child-rearing over the decade, or whether they are artifacts of the methods and samples used. Havighurst and Davis have suggested that the differences may be due to sample differences, such as ethnic or religious differences, occupational classification, or regional characteristics of the country. In regard to ethnic and religious differences, the California sample had more native-born grandparents than either the Boston or Chicago studies, and there are probably as many or more Catholics as in the Boston study[11] and fewer Jewish families. We cannot say that ethnic and religious differences are not responsible for the Chicago-Boston differences, but the fact that our

TABLE 2: *Extent of Agreement between the Three Studies of Social Class Differences*

California Social Class Findings	Agreement with Findings	
	Chicago 1943	Boston 1951–52
1. No class difference in per cent ever breast fed	Agree	Agree
2. No class difference in median duration of breast feeding (Calif. sample: Middle, 2.5 months; working, 1.5)	Agree	Agree
3. No difference in median age at completion of weaning (Calif. sample: Middle, 13.9 months; working, 12.8)	Disagree	Agree
4. No difference in number of children bottle or breast fed after 12 months	Disagree	
5. No difference in per cent of infants fed when hungry	Disagree	
6. No difference in strictness of scheduling of feeding		Agree
7. Middle class reported more thumb sucking	Agree	
8. No difference in age at which bowel training begun	Disagree	Agree
9. Working class more severe in toilet training	Agree	Agree
10. No difference in demonstrativeness of affection		Agree
11. No difference in which parent is stricter with child		Agree
12. No difference in strictness in requiring obedience		Agree
13. No difference in how much mother keeps track of child		Disagree
14. Middle class mothers report more permissiveness for aggression against parents		Agree
15. No difference in how much parent encourages child to fight back if attacked		Agree
16. No difference in permission for aggression against other children (question may not be comparable for Chicago)	Disagree	Disagree
17. No difference in severity of punishment for aggression against parents (slight difference in same direction as Boston study, but not significant)		Disagree

sample seems to be different from the Boston sample in having more native-born grandparents, more Catholics, and fewer Jews —and yet yields fairly similar results—makes less plausible any explanation depending upon these factors.

The occupational composition of the samples is not so similar as might be desired; the Boston sample contains fewer families from the lowest socioeconomic levels than does the Chicago study, and there are still fewer in the California sample. Comparability of the working class samples is, therefore, questionable, but the middle class samples in the three studies seem to be reasonably comparable, and it is here that some of the greatest differences in findings occur. Regional differences seem a less likely explanation because similar practices to those in Massachusetts were found in California within a two-year period.

Still another possibility is that our sample might contain so many women with upward mobile aspirations, even though objectively classified as working class, that class differences might be obliterated. If so, this would account for lack of agreement with the Chicago data. We were able to check this hypothesis since our sample group was asked the class they thought of themselves as belonging to—upper, lower, working, or middle. By comparing those who subjectively identify themselves as middle and working, we have one possible method of eliminating upward-mobile members of the working class from that group. There are some differences when this comparison, rather than the objective classification, is used, but the trend is still the same. In some cases, class differences are heightened.

One possible source of bias remains: both the Boston and California samples contain largely suburban respondents, families who prefer to live in residential areas and surrounding smaller towns rather than a metropolitan city. This may well be a point of difference from the Chicago sample.

This still leaves open the hypothesis that changes in child-rearing have taken place, and that differences in reference sources of the two social classes account for the differences in practices. As had been predicted, the reference sources for the two classes are different. The middle class mothers refer to more sources and to specific experts such as Spock; they are attentive to what friends and other mothers do. The working class mothers are more diffuse in approach; they "read," but no one author in particular; they seem to dip less into the larger cultural mainstream than into their own inclinations and upbringing.

Several problems present themselves before the difference in reference groups can be accepted as the cause of the differences in child rearing. The first is that this is only a partial test of the reference group hypothesis. Comparative or standard-setting reference groups have been studied rather than those with a normative function.[12] It may be that the latter are more relevant.

Secondly, although the causal relationship is plausible, it has not actually been demonstrated. It is not impossible that some other factor is responsible for the use of certain child-rearing practices and choice of reference sources. Some such factors, primarily personality variables, are suggested by the data. These are being tested and will be reported on later.

Verification of the reference group hypothesis would still not constitute evidence that a real change in practice from 1943 to 1953 had taken place.[13] Actually, this can never be demonstrated unless additional data from these years are available. If social class behavior does indeed change over time, future studies should be expected to be *unable* to replicate these results. If similar results are obtained after a ten-year period, this would be evidence against the hypothesis. If both the change and reference source hypotheses are true, then future practices of the suburban middle class should be in accord with what is being said then (or a few years earlier) in the child-rearing literature and sources of the time. These sources, incidentally, may also change.

The fact that no differences were found in the children themselves is of some interest. It may be that the measures used were insensitive. However, some of the same measures were useful and sensitive in the part of the study dealing with reaction to the birth of a sibling. It may well be that it takes longer than three or five years for class differences in the socializing process to make their mark. Perhaps it is because the majority of items reported here represent the mothers' *perceptions* of what they and the child do, and may not necessarily be descriptive of their true behavior. If the latter is so, it should be remembered that class differences in perception are an aspect of behavior worthy of study.

REFERENCES

1. Martha C. Ericson, "Social Status and Child Rearing Practices," in T. M. Newcomb and Eugene L. Hartley, eds., *Readings in Social Psychology* (New York: Holt, Rinehart, & Winston), pp. 494–501; A. Davis and R. J. Havighurst, "Social Class and Color Differences in Child Rearing," *American Sociological Review,* 11 (December 1946), 698–710. See also Robert J. Havighurst and Allison Davis, "A Comparison of the Chicago and Harvard Studies of Social Class Differences in Child Rearing," *American Sociological Review,* 20 (August 1955), 438–42.

2. Ethelyn Henry Klatskin, "Shifts in Child Care Practices in Three Social Classes Under an Infant Care Program of Flexible Methodology," *The American Journal of Orthopsychiatry,* 22 (January 1952), 52–61; Eleanor E. Maccoby and Patricia K. Gibbs and the Staff of the Laboratory of Human Development, Harvard University, "Methods of Child Rearing in Two Social Classes," in W. E. Martin and Celia Burns Stendler, eds., *Readings in Child Development* (New York: Harcourt, Brace & World, 1954); Robert R. Sears, Eleanor E. Maccoby and Harry Levin, *Patterns of Child Rearing* (New York: Harper & Row, 1957).

3. As in John W. M. Whiting and Irvin L. Child, *Child Training and Personality* (New Haven: Yale University Press, 1953), pp. 66–67.

4. David Riesman, *The Lonely Crowd* (New Haven: Yale University Press, 1950), pp. 19–23, 36–55.

5. See Martha Wolfenstein, "The Emergence of Fun Morality," *The Journal of Social Issues,* 7:4 (1951), 15–25; C. B. Stendler, "Sixty Years of Child Training Practices," *Journal of Pediatrics,* 36 (January 1950), 122–134.

6. Frances Orr, "The Reactions of Young Children to the Birth of a Sibling." More extensive information on the sample and method of obtaining it can be found here.

7. Copies of the interview and codes used in the Boston study were made available by Robert Sears.

8. W. Lloyd Warner, Marchia Meeker, Kenneth Eells, *Social Class in America* (Chicago: Science Research Associates, Inc., 1949), pp. 140–41.

9. For example, Don Lewis and C. J. Burke, "The Use and Misuse of the Chi-Square Test," *Psychological Bulletin,* 46 (November 1949), 433–89; Frederick Mosteller and Robert R. Bush, "Selected Quanti-

MARTHA STURM WHITE : 69

tative Techniques," in Gardner Lindzey, *Handbook of Social Psychology* (Reading, Mass.: Addison-Wesley, 1954), p. 314.

10. One of the most interesting differences was found on the second visit, four months later, when the children were rated on their change in psychological health. They could be rated as better, same, or worse. The middle class children were most frequently rated better or same, while the working class children were worse or same. The difference was highly significant.

11. Contrary to Havighurst and Davis, *op. cit.* (1955), p. 439, Maccoby reports in a personal communication that the Boston sample does contain Catholic children, since many do not start in parochial schools until the first grade.

12. Harold H. Kelly, "Two Functions of Reference Groups," in Guy E. Swanson, T. M. Newcomb, and Eugene L. Hartley, eds., *Readings in Social Psychology* (New York: Holt, Rinehart & Winston, 1952), pp. 410–14.

13. Indirect supporting evidence comes from a study of Evelyn Millis Duvall, "Conceptions of Parenthood," *American Journal of Sociology,* 52 (November 1946), 193–203. She found two styles of child rearing which she called *traditional,* characterized by respect and obedience, and *developmental,* characterized by emphasis on growth and development. The traditional way of thinking was more characteristic of mothers who had a child five years or older, and the developmental of those who had a child under five years. She explained this in terms of the experience of the mother—those more experienced were more strict and less flexible. However, in the light of our change hypothesis, the difference might be explained by when the mother raised the children. Those with younger children might have been more influenced by newer ideas of the 1940's while the mothers with older children might have absorbed ideas current in the late 1930's.

A study which failed to find expected changes is reported by Charles E. Ramsey and Lowry Nelson, "Change in Values and Attitudes toward the Family," *American Sociological Review,* 21 (October 1956), 605–609.

3: *A Study of Relationships between Child Rearing Attitudes and Maternal Behavior*

MICHAEL ZUNICH

Inasmuch as the literature is replete with studies concerned with the measurement of parental attitudes, there is little evidence concerning how these attitudes, as measured in the reported investigations, are related to the behavior of parents in interaction with their children. It is commonly assumed in these studies that measurements of parental attitudes yield important insights into existing parent-child relationships. The validity of such a concept, however, has not been established by empirical investigations. As Bell[1] points out, no studies directly concerned with the relation between parental attitudes and observed behavior of parents in interaction with their children have been reported in the literature. Such a study may aid psy-

Reprinted by permission of the author and publisher from *The Journal of Experimental Education*, 30 (1961), 231–41.

Some of the tables in the original article have not been included here; interested readers are referred to the issue of the journal noted above.

chologists and educators in reducing the complexity of problems involved in linking parents' attitudes to their actual behavior with their children, and may provide information on characteristics of parents which appear to affect the behavior of children.

The purpose of this investigation was to test the hypotheses that (1) maternal attitudes toward child rearing are significantly related to selected behaviors of mothers observed in interaction with their children; (2) maternal behavior is independent of social class; (3) maternal behavior is independent of the sex of the child with whom the mother interacts.

METHOD

The subjects were 80 mothers together with one of their children. Forty of the mothers were classified as lower-class and the other 40 as middle-class, according to the McGuire-White[3] index of Social Status (Short Form).

The 80 mothers meeting the following criteria, together with one of their children, served as subjects for the investigation: (1) white, (2) American born, (3) 20 to 40 years of age, (4) full-time homemakers with two or more children, and from intact families. Approximately one half of the mothers selected were observed with a male child and one half with a female child. The children ranged in age from two years and nine months to five years and one month.

Although more interaction occurs between mother and child in the home than in the laboratory, observations of mothers with their children, in this study, have been made in the laboratory setting in order to provide a control of the distracting stimuli present in homes. It was believed also that the presence of the observer in the home, where it would be difficult for him to remain unobtrusive, would influence the child's behavior to an even greater extent than would an unfamiliar setting (the laboratory) with his mother present.

The observations of middle class mothers were conducted in the Child Development Laboratory at Texas Woman's University while the lower class mothers were observed in the Child Study Laboratory at the Florida State University. Both laboratories had facilities for observing each mother together with her child through a one-way vision mirror and contained (1) various types of toys, (2) easel with paint, (3) books, (4) blocks, (5) small tables with chairs, and (6) a small kitchen unit consisting of sink, cupboard and stove.

Each mother-child pair was brought to the laboratory for one thirty-minute period for the child to play while his mother stayed in the room with him. During this visit, the mother's interaction with her child was observed and recorded according to categories similar to those developed by Merrill,[4] Bishop[2] and Schalock.[6]

The symbols, categories, and definitions were as follows:

(—) *Being Uncooperative:* Mother ignores the child's stimulation. Example: Mother continues to read magazine when child addresses her.

(c) *Contacting:* Mother is in contact with the child either verbally or physically. "Physically" means sitting or being near the child as he plays, even though she says nothing. "Verbally" means purely social conversation with the child. Example: "This is a nice dollhouse. We'll see if daddy can build one for you like it."

(n) *Criticizing:* Mother criticizes, blames, or punishes the child. Example: "Now pay attention to what you are doing. You're pouring water all over the table."

(d) *Directing:* Mother specifically states the course of action which she wants the child to follow. Example: "Put the doll over there on the table." "I want you to close the door now, Johnny, not later."

(k) *Giving Permission:* Mother consents to child's proposed activity. Example: "Yes, you may use the towel."

(m) *Giving Praise or Affection:* Mother praises or gives encouragement to the child. This category also includes expressions of affection such as petting or hugging the child. Example: "That's a very fine boat you've made."

(h) *Helping:* Mother gives physical help to the child. Example: Mother pounds a nail for the child or replaces the mast and the sail belonging to the sailboat.

(i) *Interfering:* Mother interferes with an activity on the child's part with the intent of stopping it completely. Example: "Now, now, my boy—no more of that splashing." "No, Johnny, you are not to drink the water from those cups."

(si) *Interfering by Structurizing:* Mother indicates the undesirability of a certain action and/or the consequences of the act if carried out. Example: "You know other boys and girls will want to play with those toys and if you mash them together like that they will be spoiled."

(+) *Lending Cooperation:* Mother responds to child's comments, suggestions, or requests with apparent interest and willingness. Example: "I would love to play house with you."

(a) *Observing Attentively:* Mother noticeably directs her attention to the child and/or child's activity by silently watching. Example: Mother watches child as the child plays with the stove.

(p) *Playing Interactively:* Mother is playing with the child within the framework of the child's own conception of play; she plays as though she were another child. Example: "I'll be the boat repair man and I'll fix the boat."

(z) *Reassuring:* Comfort or encouragement is offered by the mother. Example: "Don't feel too bad. Most children find it difficult to work that puzzle the first time."

(o) *Remaining Out of Contact:* Mother is sitting apart from the child, and is either reading magazines or looking away from the child. Example: Looking out of the window.

(r) *Restricting:* Mother modifies child's behavior by reducing intensity, speed, manner of executing, and so on, but does not stop activity completely. Example: "Don't splash the water so high."

(s) *Structurizing:* Mother facilitates activity on the part of the child by methods which stimulate independent thinking and relegate the responsibility of decision to the child. Example: "Do you see something in this room out of which you could make a boat?"

(t) *Teaching:* Mother gives information to the child for the purpose of increasing his knowledge. Example: "This is a duck and that is a swan. Swans have longer, thinner necks than do ducks."

RELIABILITY

Before observations were made for the purpose of data collection, it was necessary to achieve relatively high observer agreement with respect to the identification of the behavior under investigation and their accurate placement within a given time interval.

Reliability was measured by calculating percentages of agreement between two observers recording maternal behavior simultaneously during thirty-minute periods. Middle and lower class mothers together with one of their children, who were not included in the study, served as subjects for establishing reliability. The observers became familiar with the definition of behavior categories, scoring system, and code letters. Categories were memorized and agreement reached concerning types of behavior defined by each of the categories.

Measures of agreement were obtained by comparing the observations of one observer with observations taken independently and simultaneously by another observer. These measurements of agreement may be obtained by (1) computing the percentages of agreement of the observers, or (2) correlating total scores obtained by two observers in successive periods of observation. The correlation method yields a spuriously high measure of reliability in that it measures only total agreement and not agreement on identical behavior categories within specific time intervals. For this reason, the percentage method has been utilized in this study.

In utilizing a predetermined system of categories, it is difficult to determine whether disagreement between simultaneous records is a function of placing the recorded observations in the appropriate time interval or a function difference in hearing and seeing in identifying the behavior. It is possible for two observers to see different interaction occurring at the same time or to miss an event. This may be due to the position of the observers from which the interaction is viewed or in recording the behavior (looking from the behavior to the stopwatch, to the observational sheet). Also, disagreement may arise from differing interpretations of occurring interaction.

Factors such as the lack of satisfactory behavior definitions, misinterpretation of occurring behavior, and various recording methods of the observers are all factors which tend to create timing errors in the observation.

When timing errors are operating, the computation of observer agreement becomes difficult. It is impossible to determine errors or disagreements by inspection alone. If both observers have recorded the same behavior in adjacent time intervals, there is no assurance that the apparently disagreeing observations do not actually represent the same behavior. However, if both observers have the same entries in the same time interval, one cannot be certain that the agreement is not a spurious result of time differences; that is, one can never be certain that agreeing observations do not actually represent different events. The only way by which the observation can be checked is by sound photography. Since the physical settings in which observational studies are ordinarily undertaken preclude the use of necessary equipment for sound photography and because the expense makes such a technique impractical, ratings of mother-child interaction were made according to predetermined categories following a training period during which two observers demonstrated their ability to observe and record reliably. When the observers achieved a competency in the recording of the behavior represented by agreement of .80 or higher between independent observations during at least five sessions, the collection of data for the project began.

It was recognized that while the child was unaware that he was being watched, the mother might feel keenly the presence of the observer and might modify her behavior in such a manner as to present a more favorable picture of the interaction between herself and child than actually exists in the home situation. Procedures for measuring the effect of the observers' presence on the mother's behavior are being studied by other investigators, but no conclusive evidence concerning this influence is currently available.

The mother was told to imagine the time spent in the laboratory as a half hour in her own home, during which she is unoccupied by household duties and is free to be in the room where her child is playing. She was asked to act as she would if she were really in this situation. Questions were answered by stating that there was no particular way that she should act with the child and that she was free to do as she would do at home. Her behavior was rated and recorded under the appropriate category every five seconds. The observed behavior constituted the measure of the mother's behavior in interaction with her child.

THE ATTITUDE INSTRUMENT

In order to obtain measures of maternal attitudes, mothers were given the PARI developed by Schaefer and Bell.[5] This measuring instrument was selected because it offers a variety of content, assesses a wide range of attitudes, and is one upon which information concerning reliability and validity is available.

During the visit to the laboratory, the PARI was administered to the mother by the investigator after the observation session, while the child, absorbed in his play, was supervised by a graduate assistant. The administration was by means of a structured interview in a room apart from the playroom.

The items utilized in the PARI were those appearing in 16 of the 23 subscales. It was felt, because the PARI measures attitudes toward child rearing and family life, that only subscales pertaining to child rearing would be used in this study. The remaining seven subscales were concerned with attitudes toward family life.

RESULTS

Since the observations were made in two different laboratories, reliability was established for each laboratory prior to the collection of data. Disagreement most commonly evidenced by the observers was due to the placement of observed behavior in separate time intervals. This error was difficult to correct and most troublesome in establishing a satisfactory level of reliability.

The category reliabilities between the two observers, expressed in terms of per cent of their agreement concerning maternal behavior and based on ten thirty-minute periods of observation, ranged from 81 to 100 per cent.

The categories of Contacting, Directing, Observing Attentively, Remaining Out of Contact, Structurizing, and Teaching constituted the major types of the mothers' behavior toward their children while under observation. Although some mothers exhibited such behaviors as Being Uncooperative, Criticizing, and Helping, these generally had a low frequency of appearance.

Nine of the 17 behavior categories showed a significant relationship with social class at the .05 level or beyond when the median test was employed. Middle class mothers evidenced more Contacting, Directing, Helping, Interfering by Structurizing, Observing Attentively, and Playing Interactively than did lower class mothers. However, lower class mothers Remained Out of Contact more with their children than middle class mothers. In general, the middle class mothers interacted more with their children than did the lower class mothers.

Behavior categorized as Being Uncooperative, Criticizing, Giving Permission, Interfering, Interfering by Structurizing, and Playing Interactively seldom appeared in the observation of lower class mothers. Giving Praise or Affection and Reassuring were entirely lacking in the observed behavior of these mothers.

The significant relationships which appeared between the subjects' attitudes, as measured by the PARI, and their observed behavior toward their children are presented in Tables 1 and 2.

TABLE 1: *Correlation Values between Maternal Attitude Scores and Observed Behavior Ratings of Middle Class Mothers*

Attitude Subscales	Contact-ing	Direct-ing	Help-ing	Observ-ing Atten-tively	Remain-ing Out of Contact	Teach-ing
Approval of Activity	.34*			.46*		
Avoidance of Communication					.46**	
Breaking the Will		.35*				
Comradeship and Sharing			.32*			.36*
Encouraging Verbalization	.34*		.36*			.37*
Equalitarianism	.32*		.36*			.34*

* Significant at .05 level.   ** Significant at the .01 level.

TABLE 2: *Correlation Values between Maternal Attitude Scores and Observed Behavior Ratings of Lower Class Mothers*

Attitude Subscales	Directing	Lending Cooperation	Restricting
Avoidance of Communication	.34*		.46**
Breaking the Will	.34*		.46**
Encouraging Verbalization		.36*	

* Significant at .05 level.   ** Significant at .01 level.

Of the 544 comparisons made by means of Spearman rank correlation coefficients computed between frequencies in the 17 maternal behavior categories and the 16 attitude subscales, 16 evidenced significant relationships at the .05 level or beyond. Relationships are suggested by the significant values of the correlation coefficients between attitude subscales and behavior categories:

Attitude Subscales	Behavior Categories
Approval of Activity	Contacting, Observing Attentively
Avoidance of Communication	Restricting, Remaining Out of Contact
Breaking the Will	Directing, Restricting
Comradeship and Sharing	Helping, Teaching
Encouraging Verbalization	Contacting, Helping, Lending Cooperation
Equalitarianism	Contacting, Helping, Teaching

Inasmuch as one might expect, by chance, to observe values which attained significance at the .05 level approximately five times out of 100 when no real relationship exists, it would appear that interpretation of these statistical relationships should be undertaken with caution.

Middle class mothers evidenced 12 relationships between the attitude subscales and behavior categories while lower class mothers only four. It is possible that lower class mothers were shy and would not interact more freely with their children as compared with middle class mothers. However, it is not unlikely that in the home setting the middle and lower class mothers might have evidenced more Being Uncooperative, Criticizing, Interfering, and Restricting behavior, for example, than she did in the laboratory setting because of her desire to appear as a "good mother" while being observed by the experimenter. It is recognized, however, that the lack of apparent relationships may, in many instances, be a function of the setting in which the observations were made.

The frequencies of the various types of maternal contacts with sons and daughters are presented in Table 3. Of the 17 behavior categories, only five showed a significant relationship with the sex of the child at the .05 level when the median test was employed.

Two behavior categories showed a significant relationship with the sex of the child between the middle class mothers and their children. The mothers of daughters evidenced more Con-

TABLE 3: *Frequency of Maternal Contacts of Middle Class Mothers with Sons and Daughters*

| | Mothers' Interaction with | | | |
| | Sons | | Daughters | |
Behavior Categories	MC	LC	MC	LC
Being Uncooperative	4	1	2	1
Contacting	2,962	949	3,458*	1,446*
Criticizing	7	2	3	1
Directing	419	60	501	81
Giving Permission	17	—	13	2
Giving Praise or Affection	23	—	19	—
Helping	37	15	47	19
Interfering	21	4	15	4
Interfering by Structurizing	39	6	53	5
Lending Cooperation	81	18	89	17
Observing Attentively	2,989	1,500	1,699*	1,334
Playing Interactively	103	3	99	4
Reassuring	27	—	14	—
Remaining Out of Contact	605	4,528	683	4,088
Restricting	19	29	12	22*
Structurizing	61	50	72	84*
Teaching	93	57	117	70

* Median Test value significant at the .05 level.

tacting than did mothers of sons. However, mothers of sons showed more Observing Attentively behavior than did mothers with daughters.

Three behavior categories evidenced a significant relationship between lower class mothers and their children. The mothers of sons showed more Restricting behavior than did mothers with daughters. However, the mothers of daughters evidenced more Contacting and Structurizing than did mothers of sons.

DISCUSSION

The lack of statistically significant relationships observed between maternal attitudes toward children and most of the selected behavior of mothers in an unstructured laboratory setting suggests several hypotheses; that is, the mothers' behavior evidenced in a laboratory setting may not have been representative of their behavior under home conditions. Since the mother knew that an observer was present, she may have evidenced more socially acceptable behavior than is usual in the home situation.

If the experimenter obtained a reasonably close approximation of customary mother-child relationships, however, the findings suggest that maternal behavior cannot be predicted from an analysis of maternal attitudes toward children. If the mothers displayed a more socially acceptable type of interaction with the child in the laboratory than is habitual in the home, it could not be ascertained whether such behavior played a predominant role in their relationship or whether it was merely conditioned by the presence of the observer.

Since the middle class mothers interacted more with their children, the lower class mothers may have exhibited shyness or reticence in a totally unfamiliar situation. This is suggested by the low frequency of both positive and negative behaviors; that is, Being Uncooperative, Criticizing, Directing, Giving Praise or Affection, Helping, Interfering, Interfering by Structurizing, Lending Cooperation, Playing Interactively, Reassuring, Restricting, Structurizing, and Teaching. Schalock[6] states that a mother and child spend a large proportion of the time in Nonattendance and that the interaction which occurs most frequently on the part of the mother is Attendant Observation, Statement of Condition or Action, Seeking Impersonal Information, Offering Verbal Information, Directing, and Joint Participation in Activity. In the present study, such behavior makes up approximately 80 per cent of the lower class mother's interaction and 90 per cent of the middle class mother's interaction.

It would be logical to assume that middle class mothers who had children enrolled in nursery school would have a tendency to evidence less shyness or reticence and would interact more freely with their children than would mothers whose children did not attend nursery school, since mothers of nursery school children are exposed to a parent education program aimed toward increasing understanding of children and improving parent-child communication.

The data in the present study suggest several hypotheses worthy of further investigation:

In guiding their children, lower class mothers less frequently than middle class mothers (1) impose techniques of suggesting, teaching, and helping in their interaction with their children; (2) interact with their children.

In guiding their children, lower class mothers more frequently than middle class mothers (1) evidence more structurizing behavior with girls than with boys; (2) are more restrictive with boys than with girls.

Both middle class and lower class mothers more often approve than disapprove of (1) comradeship sharing between parents and their children; (2) loyalty to parents; (3) encouraging children to verbalize about their feelings without fear of reprimand; (4) equalitarianism between parents and children.

Although it is apparent that there are limitations inherent in the type of observational methodology as described in the study reported (that is, length of time required to train observers, the effect of the observer on the interaction of the subjects), such a method has several advantages when compared to others which are frequently utilized in studies of family interaction. Studies which have employed such techniques as rating scales, questionnaires, and interviews have placed, in the investigator's opinion, undue reliance upon the respondents' evaluation of the kind of interaction occurring within the family and have failed to obtain the kind of precise information which direct observation yields. Thus, the literature is replete with studies of relationships which are based upon subjective judgments of individuals who, it is generally recognized, not infrequently yield a less self-incriminating measure than would have been obtained by a trained, objective observer.

The advantage of recording behavior at the moment of occurrence in terms of yielding precise statements is obvious, yet relatively few studies have been undertaken using members of the same family in which their behavior has been rated according to predetermined categories and rated at the time of occurrence. Admittedly, such a technique is expensive in terms of the time required for the data collection. However, until such studies are undertaken in order to determine the behaviors employed by family members in their interaction with others, many of the conclusions of investigators of family behavior who have made use of the traditional questionnaire, rating scale, and interview must be considered tentative.

REFERENCES

1. Bell, R. Q., "Retrospective Attitude Studies of Parent-Child Relations," *Child Development*, 29 (1958), 323–38.
2. Bishop, B. M., "Mother-Child Interaction and the Social Behavior of Children," *Psychological Monographs*, 65:11 (1951).
3. McGuire, C., and G. D. White, "The Measurement of Social Status," *Research Paper in Human Development* (no. 3; revised; Austin: University of Texas, 1955).
4. Merrill, B. A., "A Measurement of Mother-Child Interaction," *Journal of Abnormal and Social Psychology*, 41 (1946), 37–49.
5. Schaefer, E. S., and R. Q. Bell, *Parental Attitude Research Instrument, Normative Data* (unpublished manuscript; Bethesda, Md.: Library, National Institute of Health, 1955).
6. Schalock, H. D., *Observation of Mother-Child Interaction in the Laboratory and in the Home* (unpublished doctoral dissertation; Lincoln: University of Nebraska, 1956).

4. The Deferred Gratification Pattern: A Preliminary Study

LOUIS SCHNEIDER
SVERRE LYSGAARD

Scattered pieces of sociological research have highlighted what we shall call "the deferred gratification pattern." The present paper is not primarily directed toward documentation of these bits of research, but it will gather together significant points from a number of them and will present some of the results of a preliminary empirical study designed to carry forward an exploration of the deferred gratification pattern.

Deferred gratification evidently refers to postponement of gratifications or satisfactions. Thus, in the job area, as Hollingshead shows, the lower class boy, eager to pay his own way and escape family domination, seeks a full-time job at a very early age and accordingly leaves school.[1] The freedom he thus obtains happens to be illusory and he finds himself caught in a round of

Reprinted by permission of the authors and publisher from *American Sociological Review*, 18 (April 1953), 142–49.

jobs with low pay and little promise. Deferment of the gratification of being employed and independent, through the process of obtaining a more elaborate education before one seeks a job, is eventually rewarded. But it is not necessarily implied that deferment of gratification is always worthwhile, and this is in any case largely beyond our present concern. The deferment of gratification occurs in many other areas. It may be contended that it does indeed fall into a pattern characteristic of the so-called "middle class," members of which tend to delay achievement of economic independence until after a relatively elaborate process of education, tend to defer sexual gratification through intercourse, show a relatively marked tendency to save money, and the like. For purposes of this preliminary specification, two further points must be noted. The deferred gratification pattern appears to be closely associated with "impulse renunciation."[2] Thus, some of the pertinent current literature emphasizes, by way of example, middle class renunciation of impulses toward violence. The concepts of deferment and renunciation tend, however, to overlap. One may renounce only temporarily, and the question as to whether we are dealing with renunciation or with deferment becomes verbal. A more important point is the normative character of the deferred gratification pattern. Middle class persons feel that they *should* save, postpone, and renounce a variety of gratifications. There are very probably also normative elements in the "lower class" pattern of nondeferment. Thus, Whyte notes that one of the important divergences between the social mobility pattern and the corner-boy activity pattern in Cornerville appears in matters involving expenditure of money. The college boys save money for educational purposes or to launch business or professional careers. But the corner boys must share their money with others and avoid middle class thrift. Should a corner boy have money and his friend not have it, he is expected to spend for both. The corner boy may be thrifty, but, if so, he cannot hope to hold a high position in the corner gang.[3]

Through the work of Kinsey and his associates, much clarification has been given to the deferred gratification pattern as it manifests itself in the sexual sphere. Ginzberg notes that "the poor" discount the future more heavily than "the better situated classes," and thereby, in our terms, as far as sexual intercourse is concerned, they do not defer gratification relative to "higher" classes.[4] Kinsey and his coworkers supply pertinent evidence:[5] Relatively, "lower class" persons indulge considerably in premarital intercourse; "upper class" persons show relative deferment of gratification in this sector of behavior. One illustrative comment: In two or three lower level communities it was not possible to discover a single male who had not had sexual relations with girls by the time he had reached the age of sixteen or seventeen. The rare boy who had not had such relations by that age was either physically handicapped, mentally defective, homosexual, or "earmarked for moving out of his community and going to college."[6]

Work designed to describe the pattern of deferred gratification in something like its entirety is especially marked in some of the research on Negro classes. Drake and Cayton, in probing upper class definitions of lower class life, emphasize the definition of a *pattern* of that life. They summarize some of the testimony of upper class interviewees, indicating that a few of those interviewed defined the lower class solely in terms of economic criteria, high income meaning high status, and low income low status; but that a larger number thought of a pattern, a constellation of traits, when they sought a definition of the lower class. The trait that most consistently emerged as clue to lower class status was "rowdy or indecorous behavior in public." Lower class people do not restrain their emotions and are ignorant of "how to act," of correct dress, of wise expenditure of money.[7] One gathers from the context that Drake and Cayton would largely accept the descriptive, if not the evaluative, aspects of this upper class view of the lower class pattern of life. The relevance of the description to the deferred gratification pattern is unmistakable. An earlier study by Davis and Dollard,[8] likewise of classes within a Negro community, is also highly pertinent and constituted perhaps the most immediate inspiration to the undertaking of the research reported in this paper.

The present writers proceeded on the assumption that the Davis-Dollard study might be illuminating for (at least American) class structure in general, despite its formal concern with classes in the Negro community alone. The study indicated that "impulse-following" (with minimal deferment or renunciation of "impulses" or gratifications) was characteristic of lower class Negroes and "impulse-renunciation" (or deferment of impulse-gratification) characteristic of middle class Negroes in "Old City" in the South. The study is more insightful than rigorous, and there are undoubtedly difficulties with its categorizations of class itself. Nevertheless, we may construct from it a useful listing under the general caption of the class patterning of deferred gratification. This listing served as a starting-point in our own research. The lower class characteristic of "impulse-following" (absence of deferred gratification pattern) involves: relative readiness to engage in physical violence, free sexual expression (as through intercourse), minimum pursuit of education, low aspiration level, failure of parents to identify the class of their children's playmates, free spending, little emphasis on being "'well-mannered and obedient," and short-time dependence on parents. On the other hand, the middle class characteristic of "impulse-renunciation" (presence of deferred gratification pattern) involves the reverse of these traits: relative reluctance to engage in physical violence and the like.

Admittedly, this is a rough listing and leaves us still far from a thoroughly comprehensive specification of the deferred gratification pattern. Some of the items may appear equivocal. For example, identification of class of playmates by parents perhaps does not carry on the face of it the reason for its inclusion. But it is conceived that such identification implies a concern for the maintenance of certain standards and a fear lest they be jeopardized by the contamination of "unfortunate" associations. Some items mentioned by Davis and Dollard are omitted from the list. Thus, reference is made to the "reliable middle class conscience" by contrast with the "less reliable" lower class conscience.[9] This is at a somewhat different level of abstraction from the other traits and activities noted and not so easy to handle in the type of research to be reported, and it has therefore been omitted. Finally, following Davis and Dollard, the listing tends to focus on children, but the implications plainly extend beyond them alone.

Although nothing like exhaustive documentation of the consideration of the deferred gratification pattern by sociologists has been attempted, and although we have not sought to offer anything like a finished specification of the pattern itself, the above is perhaps sufficient to suggest that the pattern deserves systematic investigation and that it is time to coordinate the bits of research endeavor that have been directed toward its study. The following preliminary and partially reported research is designed to do no more than make an appropriate step forward.

THE RESEARCH

The data utilized for the present research are based on a representative sample of 2,500 high school students. This is drawn from a larger nation-wide sample of some 15,000 high school students.[10] Although the sample, as stated, is "representative," it is not representative of all the nation's teenagers, but only of the high school population. In an investigation dealing with differential responses among *social classes,* it is, of course, of particular importance that our sample is more homogeneously middle class than the total population of high school age. The homogeneity of the sample produces an underestimate of the class differentials in the population at large. The sample does not extend adequately into the lower rungs of the stratification ladder. This probable under-representation of the lower class should serve to increase confidence in the trends actually observed.

Subjects were asked to check one of twelve occupational classes, designating the one most similar to the occupation of their fathers. These twelve occupational classifications were grouped into four occupational classes according to degree of supervisory power over "lower" occupations and independence of supervisory control from "higher" occupations. The four occupational classes follow: Class 1, Independent Occupations (including executives, directors, owners of business or farm, doctors, lawyers, bankers, ministers, professors, consulting engineers); Class 2, Dependent Occupations Involving Skill and Supervision or Manipulation of Others (including supervisors, foremen, technical engineers in industrial employment, sales workers, agents, clerks or secretaries in small businesses, teachers, nurses, preachers, reporters, public officials, entertainers); Class 3, Dependent Occupations Involving Skill but Little Supervision or Manipulation of Others (including skilled and semi-skilled workers and workers in industrial employment); Class 4, Dependent Occupations Involving Little Skill and Little Supervision or Manipulation of Others (including assembly line workers, laborers, janitors, farm workers, road workers, miners, drivers).

These occupational classes are admittedly not internally homogeneous in respect to such class criteria as "income," "prestige" or "social equality." It was intended that the classification be independent of such criteria, which at their face value might be contingent upon a certain way of life. The variable, the deferred gratification pattern (DGP), which is to be related to class affiliation is itself at least an important element of a "way of life," and we wished to avoid as far as possible the danger of obtaining an association between "class" and "response" that might turn out to be in considerable part tautological.[11]

The writers have emphasized that the occupational "classes" are not "social classes" in the sense of comprising people with clearly "common" interests, or with "class consciousness." In order to get a more "subjective" classification of our subjects we also asked them to choose one of four class designations as the one most fitting for themselves and their families: the "upper class," the "middle class," the "working class," and the "lower class."[12] It proved feasible, however, to use only "middle" and "working" class self-identifications, assimilating the very few other responses with these.

TABLE 1: *Class Self-Identification of Four Occupational Categories**

	Self-Identification		
Occupational Class	"Middle"	"Working"	TOTAL
1. Independent	80	20	100
2. Dependent, manipulative	75	25	100
3. Dependent, skilled	63	37	100
4. Dependent, unskilled	50	50	100

* Figures in percentages. Differences are significant beyond the 1 per cent level.

The poll included twenty-eight DGP-related questions. It is impossible to present all of the results here or to give them full statistical exploration. We can only affirm that our results generally give good support to the hypothesis that a class-related DGP pattern exists, especially when the self-identification index of class is used. Beyond this mere affirmation, we can present some *selected* results that are of considerable interest. Fairly typical results emerge if we follow the listing of patterns described by Davis and Dollard, and the discussion following is confined to these.

Physical Violence

The poll results show that the students who identify themselves with the "working class" report in a slightly higher proportion than those who identify themselves with the "middle class" that they have had one or more fights recently (differences significant at the 5 per cent level), that they have seen adult fights recently (differences not significant at the 5 per cent level), and that they prefer to "settle matters right away" rather than "let their temper quiet down" first (differences significant at the 1 per cent level). Slight differences are also found among the occupational classes in respect to the same questions, the lower occupational classes giving the above responses more frequently than the higher ones. The magnitude of the differences is in no case impressive, however, and we consider that these results give only slight support to the Davis-Dollard observations, as far as the occupational differentiations go.

Free Sexuality

The polling technique is not the best one for studying the sexual behavior of high school children. The poll questions had to be formulated rather vaguely because the prevalent attitudes regarding sexual matters in our high schools, and they failed to yield any clues to class differences in sexual behavior. The writers believe this failure to be accidental; it is certainly not definitive.

Marked Pursuit of Education

Data relating to education are presented in Tables 2 and 3 where the limitations of the data are evident and need no special comment. The results are nevertheless in conformity with the DGP hypothesis, although obviously they do not give conclusive proof of it.[13]

TABLE 2: *Plans after Graduation from High School of Students from Different Social Classes**

Class Index	To go to college or take special training other than college	To go to work, enlist in military service, or "other plans"	TOTAL
Self-Identification			
"Middle"	56	44	100
"Working"	42	58	100
Occupational Class			
1	62	38	100
2	61	39	100
3	48	52	100
4	32	68	100

* Figures in percentages. The chi-square test shows that differences are significant beyond the 1 per cent level for both class indices.

TABLE 3: *Expectation of Graduation from High School among Students of Different Social Classes**

Class Index	Definitely expect to graduate	Do not expect to graduate or will only "probably" graduate	TOTAL
Self-Identification			
"Middle"	80	20	100
"Working"	70	30	100
Occupational Class			
1	82	18	100
2	82	18	100
3	76	24	100
4	68	32	100

* Figures in percentages. The chi-square test shows that differences are significant beyond the 1 per cent level for both class indices.

High Aspiration Level

Students were asked on a list of twelve occupations (ranging from high to low in terms of income and prestige) to check those which they considered "not good enough" for their own life work. The higher the number thus checked, the higher the occupational aspirations of the students. Table 4 summarizes relevant data.

Identification of Class of Playmates by Parents

On the item, "My parents have definite ideas about what my friends should be like," there are small differences (not significant at the 5 per cent level) among the classes, the parents in the higher classes being reported to be more concerned about friends of children. The students themselves, however, seem to differ in respect to concern with the family backgrounds of their friends. Thus, 66 per cent of those who identify themselves with the "middle" class and 56 per cent of those who identify themselves with the "working" class (differences significant at the 1 per cent level) say that they "enjoy being together with friends

TABLE 4: *Occupational Aspirations by Social Classes**

Class Index	Median number of occupations checked as "Not Good Enough"
Self-Identification	
"Middle"	5.4
"Working"	4.8
Occupational Class	
1	5.4
2	5.3
3	5.2
4	4.9

* The difference between the medians is significant at the 1 per cent level in the case of the classes of self-identification. The median for the lowest occupational class is smaller than any of the medians of the other classes by a statistically significant amount. The differences of the medians for the upper occupational classes are not statistically significant.

who come from families at least as nice and successful as my own, rather than being together with just anybody."[14]

Free Spending

Relevant data are shown in Tables 5 and 6.

Being Well-Mannered and Obedient

This trait, or complex of traits, was examined only in the specific matter of table manners. Table 7 shows the pertinent data for the classes of self-identification but omits the data for occupational classes, for which there was no clear trend.

Prolonged Dependence on Parents

This was examined through the single indicator of savings for children, and our results are shown in Table 8.

There is little point in elaborating the many qualifications on the significance in relation to the DGP of the above data. The professional sociologist can supply some of these for himself,

TABLE 5: *Spending Preferences among High School Students of Different Social Classes**

Class Index	Spend most of it right away	Save most of it	TOTAL
Self-Identification			
"Middle"	27	73	100
"Working"	32	68	100
Occupational Class			
1	23	77	100
2	28	72	100
3	31	69	100
4	34	66	100

Responses to the question, "If you won a big prize, say two thousand dollars, what would you do?"

* Figures in percentages. The chi square test shows differences are significant beyond the 1 per cent level for both class indices.

TABLE 6: *Spending Habits among Parents of High School Students from Different Social Classes**

Class Index	Agree	Disagree	TOTAL
Self-Identification			
"Middle"	28	72	100
"Working"	43	57	100
Occupational Class			
1	16	84	100
2	32	68	100
3	39	61	100
4	45	55	100

Responses to statement, "In my family we always seem to be broke just before payday, no matter how much money is coming in."

* Figures in percentages. The chi square test shows differences are significant beyond the 1 per cent level for both class indices.

but it appears obvious that the DGP is worthy of systematic research.

Discussion

It is appropriate to add a few suggestions and questions relating to the theoretical significance of the pattern.

1. The pattern may turn out to have major significance for the "problem of order." Are there certain "advantages," certain sociopsychological "gains," that the so-called lower class has? It seems worthwhile to investigate the view that the lower class does have such advantages and reaps the "pleasure" of following impulse and not "deferring." Discounting the future, taking the cash and letting the credit go, disavowing major and worrisome self-disciplines, lower class persons may conceivably have a certain contentment that keeps them attached to an existing social order even when, from the point of view of other classes, they "live like animals."[15]

2. The pattern carries implications regarding middle class sensitivity to failure to realize rewards if the pattern is carried out uselessly. Fromm has contended, in other terminology, that

TABLE 7: *Concern for Table Manners among Parents of High School Students from Different Social Classes**

	Responses to question, "How would your parents feel if you rested your elbows on the table while eating and talked with your mouth full?"		
Class Index	They would object	They would object a little or wouldn't mind	TOTAL
Self-Identification			
"Middle"	74	26	100
"Working"	67	33	100

* Figures in percentages. The chi square test shows differences are significant beyond the 1 per cent level.

disappointment and bitterness over the very slight results achieved from adherence to the DGP among lower middle class persons in Germany after World War I were of considerable force in helping Nazism to power. "If the savings of many years, for which one had sacrificed so many little pleasures, could be lost through no fault of one's own, what was the point in saving anyway?"[16] Here again we have relevance to the problem of order. It is an old and familiar contention that jobless intellectuals are a threat to any existing social system. In more general terms, to what extent does the failure of the DGP to "pay off" mean a revolutionary reaction, or perhaps merely a private neurotic reaction? And to what extent does the pattern have functional autonomy, so that while it may have had some initial partial motivation, at any rate, in considerations of expediency alone, it cannot be sloughed off and another way of life adopted at will even when it might be convenient to be able to do the latter?

3. In view of recent interest in class mobility, it may be suggested that one fruitful line of inquiry relates to the reaction of lower class individuals toward the incipient manifestation of tendencies toward the DGP on the part of others who are lower

TABLE 8: *Savings for Children among Parents or Students from Different Social Classes**

	Students think that parents have saved money to give them a start in life.		
Class Index	Yes	No	TOTAL
Self-Identification			
"Middle"	82	18	100
"Working"	70	30	100
Occupational Class			
1	86	14	100
2	81	19	100
3	75	25	100
4	71	29	100

* Figures in percentages. The chi square test shows differences are significant beyond the 1 per cent level for both class indices.

class. Would it be possible to develop a typology on pertinent lines? We may speculate that the following types of reactions would appear: (a) A reaction of lack of comprehension, conceivably rooting at times in lack of sympathy. "What's the point of this sort of behavior?" One goes out at fourteen or thereabouts to make a living, and no fuss about it. Anything else is not understandable. This sort of reaction may well require a rather firmly stabilized lower class tradition, not susceptible to the blandishments held out, for example, by higher education. (b) A "humble" reaction. "This education business (for example) isn't for the likes of me." Here we might well anticipate anger at others from the same class because of their "pretensions." (c) A derisive reaction, on the line, "You're a sissy to study, to save, to defer."

The above can only claim to be suggestions. They are deliberately neither systematic nor comprehensive. But they point to issues which are bound to come to the fore if sociologists address themselves to serious study of the DGP.

REFERENCES

1. A. B. Hollingshead, *Elmtown's Youth* (New York: John Wiley, 1949), chapt. 14.
2. This notion, or close approximations thereto, has also cropped up frequently in recent sociological literature. See, for example, A. Davis and R. J. Havighurst, "Social Class and Color Differences in Child Rearing," in *American Sociological Review,* 11 (December 1946), 698–710.
3. W. F. Whyte, *Street Corner Society* (Chicago: University of Chicago Press, 1943), p. 106.
4. E. Ginzberg, "Sex and Class Behavior," in D. P. Geddes and E. Curie, eds., *About the Kinsey Report* (New York: The New American Library, 1948), p. 134.
5. A. C. Kinsey, W. B. Pomeroy, and C. E. Martin, *Sexual Behavior in the Human Male* (Philadelphia and London: W. B. Saunders Co., 1948), Chapt. 10.
6. *Ibid.,* p. 381. The words quoted point to what may become one of the most significant foci of study of the deferred gratification pattern—the extent to which there is early adoption by those who become upward-mobile of the class patterns of the "higher" classes, a problem given some emphasis in the work of the Warner school.
7. St. Clair Drake and H. R. Cayton, *Black Metropolis* (New York: Harper & Row, 1962), pp. 559–63. Pertinent statements or inci-

dental comments bearing directly or indirectly upon the deferred gratification pattern or its absence will be found, pp. 523, 586, 590, 592, 608, 661–62, 690, 692, 705, 714.

8. A. Davis and J. Dollard, *Children of Bondage* (Washington, D.C.: American Council on Education, 1940).

9. *Ibid.*, pp. 119 and 133.

10. The data were obtained through the Purdue Opinion Panel, Poll Number 32, administered by the Division of Educational Reference at Purdue University, Indiana. The Purdue nation-wide sample of 15,000 is fairly representative of the total high school population in the country in such factors as sex, rural-urban residence, religion, political affiliation, level of education of mothers, and house and home characteristics. The smaller sample of 2500 which we utilize has been *stratified* according to geographical region and grade in school, but strictly *randomized* from the total return of 15,000 with respect to the other characteristics listed above.

11. This points to a danger that, in general, constantly besets current class research. For example, Hollingshead's proposition that there is a functional relation between the class position of the family of an adolescent and his "social behavior" in his community (*Elmtown's Youth*, p. 441) would be more impressive if the rating procedure Hollingshead originally relies upon did not allow for the possibility that the adolescent's social behavior itself enters as an element into the determination of the class position of his family.

12. The procedure is borrowed from Richard Centers, *The Psychology of Social Classes* (Princeton: Princeton University Press, 1949), Chapt. 5. The middle class bias of our sample is indicated by the high frequency of "middle class" self-identification (about two-thirds of the subjects so identifying themselves), compared to Centers' figure for his national, male, white sample (less than one-half of the subjects identifying themselves as "middle class"). The relationship between the two classifications may be of some interest and is shown. (Since very few of our subjects marked "lower class" and "upper class" as their choice, the few "lower class" responses have been added to the "working class" category, and the "upper class" responses to the "middle class" category.)

13. In the original, more complete study, the data were analyzed for partial association; for example, the association between class of self-identification and response within each of the occupational classes, and the association between occupational class and response within each of the classes of self-identification. This analysis showed that when the variation of occupational class is accounted for there is still a significant association between class of self-identification and response. Thus, we may say that "economic opportunity," as far as that may be reflected by occupational class, is not solely responsible for the differences among the classes.

14. On this same item, there is an opposite, although not statistically significant, tendency among the occupational groups.

15. Perhaps the most fertile suggestions on this point have come from John Dollard in his *Caste and Class in a Southern Town* (New York: Harper & Row, 1949), especially Chapt. 17.

16. Erich Fromm, *Escape from Freedom* (New York: Holt, Rinehart & Winston, 1941), p. 214.

5 : The Working Class Subculture: A New View

S. M. MILLER

FRANK RIESSMAN

A decade and a half ago the working class was depicted by Allison Davis and Robert J. Havighurst[1] as permissive and indulgent toward their children and free of the emotional strain of impulse-inhibition which characterized the middle class in the United States. Indeed, it was felt by many that the middle class had much to envy and imitate in the working class.[2] This romantic view of the working class has faded. It is now asserted that the working class (usually termed the "lower class") is incapable of deferring gratification[3] and consequently unable to make major strides in improving their conditions. Frequently accompanying this view is the belief that this lower class is "immoral," "uncivilized," "promiscuous," "lazy," "obscene," "dirty," and "loud."[4] With the rising plane

Reprinted by permission of the authors and publisher from *Social Problems*, 9 (1961), pp. 86–97. The article was first presented at Annual Meetings of the American Sociological Association, New York, August 30, 1960.

99

and standard of living of workers has come the argument that workers are middle class in their outlook and desires;[5] the difficulties in attaining full middle class status lead to juvenile delinquency on the part of those youth who fall back into the working and lower classes[6] and to authoritarianism on the part of those who rise into the middle class.[7] Recently, a further vigorous blow has felled any notions of desirable characteristics of workers: their economic liberalism is not paralleled by political liberalism, for workers are said to be more authoritarian in outlook than are members of the middle class.[8] The free, spontaneous worker is now seen as an aggressive, authoritarian, yet fettered person.

The cyclothymic views of workers are more fitting as a topic in the sociology of knowledge than they are in the analysis of what workers actually believe and practice. In other work, we have criticized in some detail a number of prevailing interpretations of workers—the middle class image,[9] the nondeferred gratification pattern,[10] the authoritarian view.[11] By the nature of criticism, we have not been able to present our view of what workers are like, for they are not simply the negative or opposite of prevailing views.

For example, because it is demonstrated that workers' behavior is not consistently characterized by an inability to postpone gratifications, we cannot therefore conclude that a major characteristic of the working class is *having* a deferred gratification pattern. It may very well be that the whole issue of deferred gratification does not have special relevance to workers' lives. The concept might stem from a sociocentric point of view, where the middle class observer, in a sense, says, "If I were in the workers' boots, I wouldn't postpone gratification; I would enjoy myself while I could in the present and not worry about a future which is pretty vague and hopeless anyway." This thinking does not arise out of the context in which workers' behavior takes place, but rather is imposed upon it. In other words, the entire concept of deferred gratification may be inappropriate to understanding the essence of workers' lives.

In this paper, we can only present a few elements of what we believe is a more realistic picture of workers. This analysis is severely compressed and truncated in this presentation and it might be helpful therefore to indicate at the outset an important element of our general orientation. Our stress is much more on cognitive and structural factors than on the more commonly cited affectual and motivational ones. The nature of the conditions of working class lives (jobs, opportunities, family structure) affects behavior more than has been frequently realized; similarly, modes of understanding the environment can be more important than deep-seated personality factors in behavioral patterns. (For example, workers' low estimates of opportunities and high expectations of risk and loss may be more crucial in the unwillingness to undertake certain long-term actions than personality inadequacies involved in a presumed inability to defer gratification.) This is not to argue that motivational-psychological-affectual variables are unimportant but that they have been overstressed while cognitive and structural variables have been underemphasized. The recognition of the importance of the internal life of man has sometimes overshadowed the significance of the more manifest aspects of his existence.

Our definition of working class is simple: regular members of the nonagricultural labor force in manual occupations. Thus, we exclude the "lower class," irregular working people, although the analysis has some relevance to the lower class, as will be mentioned below. One of the greatest sources of difficulties in understanding nonupper and nonmiddle class behavior is that social scientists have frequently used the omnibus category of "lower class" to encompass the stable, and frequently mobile, fairly high income skilled workers, the semiskilled factory worker, the worker in varied service trades, the unskilled worker and the irregular worker. This collection is probably more a congeries of fairly disparate groups than a category with similar life chances and circumstances. It is especially important to distinguish the segment which has irregular employment (and "voluntary" withdrawals from the labor force), unskilled jobs in service occupations (and is largely Negro and Puerto Rican now) from the other groupings, which are larger and have more of a commonness to them.

This latter group of regular workmen we call "working class" despite the reluctance of many social scientists today to use this historic term; the opprobrious term "lower class" might be applied to the irregular segment, although it would probably be better all around if a less invidious term (perhaps "the unskilled") were employed.

The reluctance to make the distinction between "working class" and "lower class," despite useful discussions by Kahl[12] and others, not only is a topic worthy of independent study, but leads to error. For example, Hollingshead and Redlich in their important study have been interpreted as finding that the lower the class, the higher the rate of mental illness. Close examination of their data reveal, however, that the working class, Class IV, is closer to the upper and middle classes, Classes I, II and III, than to the lower class, Class V. Classes I through IV are similar, while Class V is quite dissimilar from all the other classes, including the working class.[13]

Within the working class, we are primarily interested in the *stable* working class subculture. We believe there is considerable variation within the working class,[14] but the differences probably are variations upon the theme of the stable working class pattern. While we think in terms of working class subcultures, and, to some extent, lower class subcultures, a key to understanding them, we believe, is likely to be the *stable* working class subculture.

PHENOTYPES, GENOTYPES, AND THE MIDDLE CLASS

Our analysis is aimed at developing *themes* in working class life. Thus, we are interpreting the *meaning* of findings rather than reporting new findings. We have utilized the published materials commonly employed plus our own interviews and observations of working class people.

A major inadequacy in explanations of the working class life style has been the failure to explain behavior in terms of genotypes. For example, in attitudinal polls in which similar questions are asked of middle and working class people, many differences are revealed between the two groups. But what is the meaning of the replies? For example, if workers agree with the statement, "'Communists should be imprisoned," does it mean that they are especially unaccepting of civil liberties or that they are punitive toward those whom they see as criminals, and that they consider punishment an effective deterrent and a just reward for wrongdoing? They may be wrong in all respects, but does their attitude reflect fundamentally a rejection of Bill of Rights thinking or a punitive attitude which has as one of its results in a specific situation the denial of civil liberties? Emphasis on the phenotype, civil liberties, may obscure the basic dynamics of the attitude in stressing a Bill of Rights little known to workers.[15]

Another illustration of phenotypic analysis was the tendency of Davis and Havighurst to denote long breast-feeding as belonging in the cluster they termed permissive child care. This may have been accurate for the middle class since long breast-feeding is associated there with the *ideology* of permissiveness: indulgence, reliance on love, child-centered, and so on. It is not for the working class because long breast-feeding is not related genotypically to the permissive child-rearing *ideology* in that class.[16]

A second major difficulty in explaining working class life is the preoccupation with comparing it with the middle class.[17] The comparisons have perhaps inevitably a pejorative tone so that, for example, at one time those critical of the middle class could charge it with having poor child care compared to the more spontaneous workers. It appears that some of the critics of this view have moved to the other pejorative extreme and are now critical of working class child care and rather uncritically praising of the middle class style of child care.[18]

A difficulty then in analyzing the working class has been this value shift to a more positive orientation toward the middle class and therefore a more critical view of the working class. As one class ascends in approval the other descends, because the two classes are seen in a contrapuntal and judgmental relationship.

Another difficulty is that the middle class has apparently changed considerably in various ways so that comparisons involving the middle class are frequently of official norms rather than actual practices, of old norms rather than present norms. For example, it is frequently said that many working class children of talent do not go on to college because they lack the ability to defer gratification, an ability the college-bound middle class youth displays. Is it really true today in the prosperous middle class youth culture of the United States that most middle class youth are deferring gratification when they go to college? More likely, many look upon it in anticipation and retrospect as coming closest in their total experiences to the realization of gratifications.[19] Frequently, it seems that the working class is compared with an inner-directed, economically marginal middle class of yore than with an "acting-out," "other-directed," "affluent" middle class of today. The shifts in the middle class, murky as they are, make it especially difficult and dubious to use it as a yardstick for elucidating (and frequently evaluating) working class life.

BASIC THEMES

Before discussing a few of the themes which we think are basic in working class life, we present a brief overall picture of what we believe are the essential characteristics of the stable American worker today.

He is traditional, "old fashioned," somewhat religious, and patriarchal.[20] The worker likes discipline, structure, order, organization and directive, definite (strong) leadership, although he does not see such strong leadership in opposition to human, warm, informal, personal qualities.[21] Despite the inadequacy of his education, he is able to build abstractions, but he does so in a slow, physical fashion.[22] He reads ineffectively, is poorly informed in many areas, and is often quite suggestible, although interestingly enough he is frequently suspicious of "talk" and "new fangled ideas."

He is family centered; most of his relationships take place around the large extended, fairly cooperative family.[23] Cooperation and mutual aid are among his most important characteristics.[24]

While desiring a good standard of living, he is not attracted to the middle class style of life with its accompanying concern for status and prestige.[25]

He is not class conscious, although aware of class differences. While he is somewhat radical on certain economic issues, he is quite illiberal on numerous matters, particularly civil liberties and foreign policy.[26]

The outstanding weakness of the worker is lack of education. Strongly desiring education for his children, he shows considerable concern about their school work, although he feels estranged and alienated from the teacher and the school, as he similarly feels alienated from many institutions in our society.[27] This alienation is expressed in a ready willingness to believe in the corruptness of leaders and a general negative feeling toward "big shots."

He is stubborn in his ways, concerned with strength and ruggedness, interested in mechanics, materialistic, superstitious, holds an "eye for an eye" psychology, and is largely uninterested in politics.

Stability and Security

We suspect that one of the central determinants in working class life is the striving for stability and security.[28] External and internal factors promote instability and insecurity. Chief among the external factors is unemployment and layoff. Prosperity has of course barred the anguish of the prolonged depression of the

1930's, but the danger of occasional layoffs of some duration are not remote during the usually shaky prosperity conditions, which are interlarded with episodes of recession, plant relocation, industry decline, and strikes.[29]

Chief among the internal factors promoting instability are family discord, including divorce and desertion, intergenerational conflict, and the desire for excitement.

Coping with the instability threats becomes a dominant activity within the working class family. Many practices, such as mutual aid and cooperation, extended family perspectives, are important as adjustive mechanisms. "Getting by" rather than "getting ahead" in the middle class self-realization and advancement sense is likely to be dominant.[30] For example, the limited desire to become foremen is partly a result of the economic insecurity resulting from the loss of job seniority in case of a layoff.[31]

Part of the ambivalence toward obtaining a college education reflects the same emphasis on security. Even a highly talented working class youth is not sure what he can do with a college diploma, and he may fear the disruption of his familial, community and peer group security.[32]

The poll data indicating the unwillingness of workers to take economic risks and their greater concern for jobs with security is part of the same pattern of a striving for stability.[33]

Traditionalism

The American working class is primarily a migrant group; not only have people come from European farms and rural settlements to American factories but they also have migrated from America's rural life to the industrial scene.[34] Traditional practices, once thought to be infrequent in urbanized, industrialized, nuclear-oriented families, are very strong in working class families.[35] The pattern is patriarchal, extended (with many relevant cousins, grandparents, and aunts and uncles) and delineated by sharply separated sex roles. The family is not child-centered (or child-dominant or dominating), but parent-

centered and controlled. Traditional values of automatic obedience by children are expected to be the norm even if not always
observed in practice.[36]

One probable consequence of this is that workers seem to be
more authoritarian than they probably are. For while on the
F-scale type of test, they tend to be "conventional," a characteristic of the authoritarian, according to Adorno *et al.*, it is
doubtful, as we have tried to argue elsewhere,[37] that this con-
ventionalism means the same in both the middle and working
class.

The worker also has a traditional attitude toward discipline
which again may be confused with authoritarianism. All the
child-rearing data indicate that workers utilize physical punishment as a basic discipline technique. In the eyes of the worker
punishment discourages people from wrong-doing whether the
punishment is inflicted upon them or upon others who serve
as "examples." There is also a "rightness" about punishment
for a misdeed, for punishment is the other side of responsibility
for one's actions. Thus, for example, acceptance of the death
penalty may not be the result of a sado-masochistic character
structure but the product of a belief in the efficacy of punishment in deterring others from misdeeds and in the value of
attaching responsibility to people's actions.[38] Workers consequently do not easily accept the notion that an individual is not
responsible for his crimes because of his emotional state at the
time of their occurrence.

Intensity

We believe that one of the most neglected themes in working
class life and one of the most difficult to understand and interpret is that of intensity. This intensity is expressed in a number
of different ways. It is found in the areas in which workers have
belief and emotional involvement. While there are numerous
areas about which workers are confused, and lacking in opinion
(for example, the high percentage of "no answer" and "don't
know" on public opinion polls), there are important spheres in

which they have definite convictions, and indeed, are highly stubborn. Their beliefs about religion, morality, superstition, diet, punishment, custom, traditional education, the role of women, intellectuals, are illustrative here. Many of these attitudes are related to their traditional orientation and they are held unquestioningly in the usual traditional manner. They are not readily open to reason and they are not flexible opinions.

Other possible sources of this intensity may be their physical (less symbolic) relation to life,[39] their person-centeredness (to be discussed below), and their lack of education.

Person-Centered

Threaded through much of working class life is a person-centered theme. On one level this theme has an informal, human quality of easy, comfortable relationships with people where the affectionate bite of humor is appreciated. The factory "horse play," the ritualistic kidding, is part of this although by no means all of it. It is an expressive component of life.[40]

At another level, it is the importance of personal qualities. One learns more from people than from books, it is said. At a political level, the candidate as a decent, human person is more important than the platform.[41]

In the bureaucratic situation, the worker still tends to think of himself as relating to people, not to roles and invisible organizational structure. This orientation is an aspect of particularism, the reaction to persons and situations in terms of their personal qualities and relations to oneself rather than in terms of some universal characteristics of their social position. The neighbor or workmate who gets ahead is expected "not to put on airs"; he should like the "old gang" and accept them despite his new position. An individual is expected to transcend his office. A foreman is a s.o.b. not because he has stresses and demands on the job which force him to act forcibly and harshly, but because of his personal qualities. Contrariwise, one of the top executives is frequently regarded as one who would help the rank-and-file workers if he had the chance, because *he* is a "nice guy"; putting him in the stresses of a new position would not force him to act as others in that position have acted.[42] It is the man, not the job, that makes for behavior; this attitude is not a class conscious one, far from it. Another example of particularism is the juvenile delinquent who reacts positively to the social worker or therapist who seems to be interested in him beyond the call of professional duty.

Pragmatism and Anti-Intellectualism

With workers, it is the end result of action rather than the planning of action or the preoccupation with means that counts. An action that goes astray is not liked for itself; it has to achieve the goal intended to be satisfactory.[43] It is results that pay off. While this orientation has an anti-intellectual dimension, it does somewhat reduce the reliance on personality (person-centered theme) by its emphasis on results. Workers like the specific action, the clear action, the understood result. What can be seen and felt is more likely to be real and true in the workers' perspectives, which are therefore likely to be limited. The pragmatic orientation of workers does not encourage them to see abstract ideas as useful. Education, for what it does for one in terms of opportunities, may be desirable, but abstract intellectual speculation, ideas which are not rooted in the realities of the present, are not useful, indeed may be harmful.

On the other hand, workers often have an exaggerated respect for the ability of the learned. A person with intellectual competence in one field is frequently thought to be a "brain" with ability in all fields; partly this is due to the general abstract nature of ideas regardless of field. If a real obstacle comes up, they may expect "the brain" to have a ready solution for it, even if they may not be willing to adopt it.

At first glance, the anti-words orientation may appear to be incompatible with the possible appeal of the charismatic. But it is not. For the charismatic are charismatic because they can be emotional and expressive, qualities not usually associated with abstract ideas. Also, the charismatic leader may promise "pie in the sky," but it is a very concrete, specific set of ingredients with a clear distribution of the pie.

Excitement

Another component in workers' lives is the appreciation of excitement, of moving out of the humdrum. News, gossip, new gadgets, sports, are consequently very attractive to workers. To some extent, the consumership of workers—the desire to have new goods, whether television sets or cars—is part of this excitement dimension. The excitement theme is often in contradiction with the traditional orientation.

It is worth noting that different subgroups within the working class may favor one theme rather than another. Thus, younger groups, and especially juvenile delinquents, are probably much more attracted to the excitement theme, are more alienated and less traditional. On the other hand, workers with a more middle class orientation are probably less alienated, more traditional and pragmatic.

Parsimony and Variation

In the preceding remarks we have touched only very fleetingly on a few themes of working class life and ignored other important themes, like cooperation and a physical orientation, almost completely. While we can sum up our analysis in a relatively few descriptive adjectives, such as person-centered, traditional, pragmatic, and so on, we have been unable to develop a parsimonious conceptualization, such as a nondeferred gratification pattern which attempts to explain by this single formulation or theme a vast array of behavior. Perhaps the simplest shorthand, if one wishes to use it, would be Parsons'; employing his criteria, we could say that workers are particularistic rather than universalistic, affective rather than neutral, ascriptive rather than achievement-minded, diffuse in definition of role rather than specific. But this summary may obscure more than it reveals.

Indeed, our analysis contains a number of themes which may, in part, be in opposition to each other. For example, traditionalism and alienation have certain conflicting features, as do pragmatism and person-centeredness, and the resulting strains and adjustive mechanisms are important to analyze.

Let us make just two points to indicate the general value of the orientation that we have only sketchily presented here. (1) It may be possible to understand other working class and lower class styles by looking for sources of variation from the stable working class pattern. (2) The development of the stable working class style among lower class and working class youth might be the goal of educational and other socializing and remedial forces rather than the instilling of the middle class value structure.

Variations of Working Class Culture

By stating that we are describing the *stable* worker we imply that there are other worker subcultures. We feel that the stable worker has been relatively ignored in the emphasis on the "underprivileged," "lower class," unskilled, irregular worker and the middle class oriented worker. By understanding the stable worker, important leads are provided for understanding other subcultural variations.

The unskilled, irregular (read "lower class") worker lacks the disciplined, structured, and traditional approach of the stable worker and stresses the excitement theme. He does less to cope with insecurity and instability. In the large industrial and commercial centers today the lower class style of life (as distinct from the stable working class style) is found particularly among peoples relatively new to industrial and urban life: Negroes, Puerto Ricans, transplanted Southern whites. They have not been able so far to make the kind of adjustment that stable workers have. Frequently, they have special problems not only of discrimination but of fairly menial (service) jobs at low pay, extremely poor housing and considerable overcrowding. Some children of stable workers do not develop the stable pattern and assume the lower class style. A few children of middle class parents become lower class: They have un-skilled jobs and adopt the lower class style of life. But the bulk of individuals with the lower class style come from those who are children of unskilled workers and of farmers, thus including many of the ethnic people of whom we spoke earlier.[44]

Another deviant group from the main working class pattern are those workers who are very much concerned with achieve-ment of success for children and for the symbols of success in consumership. In many cases the families are secure and stable and have been able to make a workable accommodation to the stresses of their lives. But this is not enough for the middle class orientation; in many cases there is a vague opportunity and motivational factor present.

Those of working class origins who do move into the middle class and into the middle class style of life are likely to have a middle class cross-pressure in that they more frequently than other working class children have relatives who were or are middle class. Their grandparents may have been middle class; their parents though in working class occupations are more likely to have more education than is typical in the working class and to have other attributes of middle class life.[45] If we may give a literary example, in *Sons and Lovers,* the hero, brought up in a mining community, had a working class father but his mother was a teacher and came from a middle class community. Undoubtedly, the hero, whose life follows that of D. H. Lawrence, received motivation from her to move into literary activities and probably also some early direct help in reading and school. The motivational factor is important but it is likely linked to the background and experiential factor of grandparental and paternal activities.

We have discussed these two styles in different ways. The lower class style is considered to be the inability to develop an adequate measure of coping with the environment so that some degree of security and stability ensues. The origin of the middle class style would seem to emerge from the stable pattern. A working class family would likely first go through a stable period of accommodation before it or the children developed middle class orientations. *It is not intrinsic in the stable pattern that a middle class orientation emerge, but the stable stage would seem to be a necessary step in most cases for the development of a middle class orientation.*

Other variations in the subculture of workers exist. Religious, ethnic, educational, and regional factors are important in producing deviations from the pattern we have described.

THE STABLE STYLE AS GOAL

Explicitly as well as implicitly, many agents of educational and other institutions that deal with working class and lower class youth attempt to "middle classize" them. When any effort is extended toward the juvenile delinquent, it is usually with this orientation. Such endeavors are largely a failure because the middle class outlook is alien to the experiences, prospects and values of these youth. Possibly there is a better chance of emphasizing working class values: for example, cooperation— as happens in group therapy—rather than vocational success in middle class terms. We recognize that it is not easy to develop some of the working class values but they are probably much easier to develop than the middle class ones. In addition, emphasis on the former may develop a more favorable attitude on the part of the youth to both the institution and its agents than does the insistence on the middle class values.

A basic value question is involved here: Do we attempt to make the middle class style a model for all to follow? Or do we adopt a rigid cultural relativity position that the lower class has a right to its way of life regardless of the social effects? Or do we attempt to develop what appear to be the most positive elements, from the point of view of society and the individuals involved, of the styles of life closest to them? While we have some doubts about the answer, the possibility of the stable working class style as the goal adds a new dimension to a deep problem that deserves more forthright scrutiny than it has received.

Our attempts at interpreting working class life will undoubtedly prove inadequate. But we are certain that without an attempt at analyzing the contexts and the genotypes of working class behavior and attitude, the *description* (and there is faulty description) and interpretation of working class life will remain a reflex of social scientists' changing attitudes toward the middle class.

REFERENCES

1. Allison Davis and Robert J. Havighurst, "Social Class and Color Differences in Child Rearing," *American Sociological Review*, 11 (December 1946), pp. 698–710.
2. See David Riesman in his introduction to Ely Chinoy's *American Workers and Their Dreams* (Garden City, N.Y.: Doubleday, 1955).
3. Louis Schneider and Sverre Lysgaard, "The Deferred Gratification Pattern: A Preliminary Study," *American Sociological Review*, 18 (April 1953), 142–49.
4. These adjectives are taken from Rodman, who then goes on to declare: "Lantz, Centers, Warner, *et al.*, Hollingshead, Drake and Cayton, West, and David, Gardner and Gardner make it clear that this is the way the lower class is viewed within the United States; the Henriques and Braithwaite studies make it clear that this is the way the lower class is viewed within the West Indies." Hyman Rodman, "On Understanding Lower-Class Behaviour," *Social and Economics Studies*, 8 (December 1959). Other authors state: "One of the most venerable stereotypes has been that applied by middle class people to lower class people. The qualities have from time to time included lack of thrift, intellectual inferiority, habitual dirtyness, licentiousness, and many that have derogatory implications." Robert R. Sears, Eleanor E. Maccoby, and Harry Levin, *Patterns of Child Rearing* (New York: Harper & Row, 1957), p. 442. We have isolated five types of stereotypes of workers—anomic, depraved, incapable of deferring gratification, class conscious and middle class oriented; these are discussed in S. M. Miller and Frank Riessman, "Images of Workers," a paper presented to the Eastern Sociological Society, New York, 1957.
5. Daniel Bell, *The End of Ideology* (New York: The Free Press, 1959), and in various issues of *Fortune* magazine. On the other hand, see his path-breaking article, "The Subversion of Collective Bargaining," *Commentary* (March 1960).

6. Albert Cohen, *Delinquent Boys: The Culture of the Gang* (New York: The Free Press, 1955).

7. Joseph Greenblum and Leonard I. Pearlin, "Vertical Mobility and Prejudice: A Sociopsychological Analysis," in Reinhard Bendix and Seymour Martin Lipset, eds., *Class, Status and Power* (New York: The Free Press, 1953).

8. Seymour Martin Lipset, *Political Man: The Social Bases of Politics* (Garden City, N.Y.: Doubleday, 1960), chapt. 4.

9. S. M. Miller and Frank Riessman, "Are Workers Middle Class?" *Dissent* (Fall 1961).

10. S. M. Miller and Frank Riessman, "The Nondeferred Gratification Pattern: A Critique," unpublished.

11. S. M. Miller and Frank Riessman, " 'Working-Class Authoritarianism': A Critique of Lipset," *British Journal of Sociology,* forthcoming.

12. Joseph A. Kahl, *The American Class Structure* (New York: Holt, Rinehart & Winston, 1959), pp. 205 *ff.*

13. For the original report, see A. B. Hollingshead and Frederick C. Redlich, *Social Class and Mental Illness* (New York: John Wiley, 1958). The point above is taken from S. M. Miller and Elliot G. Mishler, "Social Class, Mental Illness, and American Psychiatry," *Milbank Memorial Fund Quarterly,* 38 (April 1959), 174–99.

14. Robert Blauner, in his thoughtful paper, "Industrial Differences in Work Attitudes and Work Institutions," points out important differences among workers in different industries. Bennett Berger, *Working Class Suburb* (Berkeley: University of California Press, 1960) believes there are differences in attitudes among workers of "Arkie" and "Okie" backgrounds, and workers of a nonrural background. A variety of studies show the importance of educational differences among workers, a factor with which we are very concerned. See Frank Riessman, *Workers' Attitudes towards Participation and Leadership* (unpublished Ph.D. dissertation in social psychology; New York: Columbia University, 1955).

15. See David Joseph Bordua, *Authoritarianism and Intolerance, A Study of High School Students* (unpublished Ph.D. thesis, Department of Social Research; Cambridge: Harvard University, 1956), pp. 228, 237, 239.

16. Evelyn Millis Duvall, "Conceptions of Parenthood," *American Journal of Sociology,* 52 (November 1946)), 193–203. See also Martha Wolfenstein, "The Emergence of Fun Morality," *Journal of Social Issues,* 7:4 (1951), 15–25.

17. Hyman Rodman, *op. cit.*

18. See Urie Bronfenbrenner, "Socialization and Social Class through Time and Space," in E. E. Maccoby, T. M. Newcomb and R. L. Hartley, eds., *Readings in Social Psychology* (New York: Holt, Rinehart & Winston, 1958).

19. Some of us who have been through the mill of graduate school may feel, as suggested to us by Harold Wilensky, that we, at least, have deferred gratification! On the other hand, Allison Davis' discussion of "the graduate or medical student who is largely dependent upon his own earnings . . ." is certainly out-of-date for at least the medical student. Allison Davis, "Socialization and Adolescent Personality," in G. E. Swanson, T. M. Newcomb and E. L. Hartley, eds.,

Readings in Social Psychology (New York: Holt, Rinehart & Winston, 1952), p. 530.

20. The cross-class F-scale studies uniformly show that workers are more likely than middle class individuals to support the statement that "the most important thing a child should learn is obedience to his parents." Maccoby and Gibbs have pointed out that workers strongly demand respect and obedience from their children. Eleanor E. Maccoby, Patricia K. Gibbs, *et al.*, "Methods of Child Rearing in Two Social Classes," in William E. Martin and Celia Burns Stendler, eds., *Readings in Child Development* (New York: Harcourt, Brace & World, 1954), pp. 380–96. Riessman's data indicate that not only parents but older people in general are to be obeyed and respected. See Frank Riessman, *op. cit.*, and Duvall, *op. cit.*

21. Frank Riessman, *op. cit., passim.*

22. For a review of the relevant literature, see Frank Riessman, *Education and the Culturally Deprived Child* (New York: Harper & Row, 1961).

23. Floyd Dotson, "Patterns of Voluntary Association Among Urban Working Class Families," *American Sociological Review,* 16 (October 1951), 687–93. "In at least 15 of the 50 families, leisure time activities of the husbands and wives were completely dominated by the kin group. In another 28 families, regular visiting patterns with relatives constituted a major, although not exclusive, form of social activity (p. 691). See also p. 693.

24. August B. Hollingshead, "Class Differences in Family Stability," in Bendix and Lipset, *op. cit.*, p. 290. A similar point is made by Allison Davis, Burleigh B. Gardner, and Mary R. Gardner, *Deep South* (Chicago: University of Chicago Press, 1941), p. 111. See also John Useem, Pierre Tangent, and Ruth Useem, "Stratification in a Prairie Town," *American Sociological Review,* 7 (June 1942), 334.

25. The relevant literature is discussed in Miller and Riessman, "Are Workers Middle Class?" *op. cit.*

26. The Centers' findings can be interposed to support the first sentence of the paragraph despite Centers' mode of analysis. Richard Centers, *The Psychology of Social Classes* (Princeton: Princeton University Press, 1949). See also Ralf Dahrendorf, *Class and Class Conflict in Industrial Society* (Stanford: Stanford University Press, 1959), pp. 288–289. On civil liberties and foreign policy, see Lipset, *op. cit.*

27. Riessman, *Education and the Culturally Deprived Child*, has a discussion of some of the relevant literature.

28. Hollingshead, *op. cit.*, pp. 290–1.

29. Charles H. Hession, S. M. Miller and Curwen Stoddart, *The Dynamics of the American Economy* (New York: Knopf, 1956), Chapt. 11.

30. Joseph A. Kahl, *op. cit.*, pp. 205–210.

31. Ely Chinoy, *op. cit.*, and Charles R. Walker, *Steeltown* (New York: Harper & Row, 1950) have data showing the considerable reluctance of workers to become foremen.

32. The initial attraction of many working class youth to engineering is partly due to the apparently concrete and clear nature of the work and the presumed definiteness of the education for a particular type of job. Motivating working class youth to go to college may require

an expansion and sharpening of working class children's interpretation of the job market.

33. Centers, *op. cit.*, p. 62.
34. Lloyd Reynolds, *Labor Economics and Labor Relations* (Englewood Cliffs, N.J.: Prentice-Hall, 1949), pp. 7–23.
35. Recent literature, particularly Weinstein and Axelrod, have pointed out that traditional practices are more widespread than previously thought in the middle class. The lack of differences between middle class and working class respondents reported in the studies may be due to the lack of sensitive instruments. While our analysis is not necessarily based on the notion of greater traditional and extended practices in working class than in middle class families, we believe that these practices assume a greater importance in the over-all activities of the former.
36. Duvall, *op. cit.*
37. Miller and Riessman, " 'Working-Class Authoritarianism': A Critique of Lipset," *op. cit.* Also, our "Social Class, Education and Authoritarianism," a paper presented to the American Sociological Society, Washington, D.C., 1957.
38. See Bordua, *op. cit.*
39. The discussion by Miller and Swanson on the "motoric" orientation of workers is one of the most suggestive in the literature: Daniel R. Miller and Guy E. Swanson, *Inner Conflict and Defense* (New York: Holt, Rinehart & Winston, 1960).
40. *Ibid.*
41. See Lipset, *op. cit.*, pp. 285–86.
42. S. M. Miller, *Union Structure and Industrial Relations: A Case Study of a Local Labor Union* (unpublished Ph.D. thesis; Princeton: Princeton University, 1951).
43. Melvin L. Kohn, "Social Class and the Exercise of Parental Authority," *American Sociological Review,* 24 (June 1959), 364–65.
44. The data to support this assertion can be computed from the two American studies detailed in the appendix to S. M. Miller, "Comparative Social Mobility," *Current Sociology* (1961).
45. See the remarks of Kaare Svalastoga in "Report of the Fifth Working Conference on Social Stratification and Social Mobility" of the International Sociological Association, 1960.

6: *Some Aspects of Lower Class Sexual Behavior*

LEE RAINWATER

The belief that the price of increasing affluence and sophistication (at least through the middle ranges) is loss of the ability to act and feel as a "natural man" has long been a part of the American cultural tradition. Confounded in the complex myths which express this belief are natural virtue, innocence, honesty, love, fun, sensuality, and taking pleasure where and how one can find it. Natural man as hero can be constructed by any selection of these characteristics; some versions emphasize virtue and innocence, others emphasize fun, sensuality and pleasuring oneself. But to our Puritan minds natural man can also be evil; we have myths of naturalness that emphasize immorality, hatefulness, sexual avarice, promiscuity, and sensual gluttony. Many of the images which Ameri-

Reprinted by permission of the author and publisher from *Journal of Social Issues*, 22 (1966), 96–107.

cans have, and historically have had, of the lower class can be subsumed under one or another version of natural man as good or evil. Whatever the evaluative overtones to a particular version of these myths, they add up to the fact that the lower classes (like racial and ethnic minorities, primitive peoples, Communists, and others) are supposed to be gaining gratifications that more responsible middle class people give up or sharply limit to appropriate relationships (like marriage) and situations (like in bed and at night.) * These contrasting themes of naturalness as good and naturalness as evil are really mutually reinforcing, since they support the view that "naturalness" exists and is defined by the common terms of the two themes— and *pari passu* that "unnaturalness" exists and is defined by the absence of these two themes.†

An article dealing with lower class sexual behavior would be expected, then, to describe a group of happy or God-forsaken sinners who derive a great deal more sexual gratification in their society than do middle class respectables in theirs. However, the little empirical research which examines lower class sexual behavior—and, more important, lower class subjective responses to sex—tends to support quite a different view.‡ Since we have fuller comparative information on sexual

---

* John Dollard has analyzed some of the attitudes that white Southerners have toward Negroes, which compound both the positive and negative views of lower status naturalness. In his analysis he perhaps took somewhat too seriously the notion that lower class Negroes gain from the greater sexual freedom allowed them by the caste system.[6] Allison Davis, an insufficiently appreciated pioneer in the study of lower class cultures, seems to have been similarly taken in by the myth: "In the slum, one certainly does not have a sexual partner for as many days each month as do middle class married people, but one gets and gives more satisfaction over longer periods, when he does have a sexual partner" (p. 33).[5]

† Kai Erikson[7] in an analysis of the functions of deviance and its control in the establishment of social boundaries comments, "Every culture recognizes a certain vocabulary of contrasts which are meant to represent polar opposites on the scale of human behavior . . . [but] when we look across the world to other cultures . . . or behind us to the historical past, it often seems that these contrasting forms are little more than minor variations on a single cultural theme."

‡ The shift to a more jaundiced view of the happy impulse-free version of lower class sexual life is paralleled by a similar shift in the under-

relations within marriage for lower, working, and middle class couples, we will examine sex within the context of marriage first.

MARITAL SEXUALITY IN THE LOWER CLASS

At all class levels, marital sexual relations provide the major source of sexual outlet for most men and women during their sexual careers. In all social classes, also, marital and sexual relations are considered the preferable and most desirable outlet. Other sources of outlet are most often seen by their seekers as compensations or substitutes rather than really preferable alternatives. We start, then, with a comparison of the ways husbands and wives in the lower, working, and middle classes evaluate marital sexuality, the attitudes they have toward sexual relations, and the gratifications and dissatisfactions they find in these.

The material that follows is drawn from a larger study,[18, 20] which examines marital sexuality as part of the family context for family size decisions and family limitation behavior. The study is based on interviews with 409 individuals—152 couples, and 50 men and 55 women not married to each other. Thus, 257 families are represented. The respondents lived in Chicago, Cincinnati, or Oklahoma City, and were chosen in such a way as to represent the social class range of whites from upper-middle to lower-lower and Negroes at the upper-lower and lower-lower class levels.

---

standing of lower class delinquency. Bordua, in comparing the work of Frederick Thrasher in the 1920's with that of Walter Miller, Albert Cohen, Richard Cloward, and Lloyd Ohlin, comments, "All in all, though, it does not seem like much fun any more to be a gang delinquent. Thrasher's boys enjoyed themselves being chased by the police, shooting dice, skipping school, rolling drunks. It was fun. Miller's boys do have a little fun, with their excitement[2] focal concern, but it seems so desperate somehow. Cohen's boys and Cloward and Ohlin's boys are driven by grim economic and psychic necessity into rebellion. It seems peculiar that modern analysts have stopped assuming that 'evil' can be fun and see gang delinquency as arising only when boys are driven away from 'good' " (p. 136).[1]

Men and women were asked to discuss their feelings about their sexual relations in marriage, the gratifications they found, the dissatisfactions they had, the meaning of sex in their marriage, and the importance it had to them and to their spouses.

One dimension emerging from the answers to all of these questions can be thought of as a continuum of interest and enjoyment in sexual relations, which ranges from very great interest and enjoyment to strong rejection. The range is most apparent among women, of course; men only rarely say they are indifferent to or uninterested in sexual relations, but women present the gamut of responses from "If God made anything better, He kept it to Himself," to "I would be happy if I never had to do that again; it's disgusting." On the basis of each individual's response to all of the questions about sexual relations, he was classified as showing either great or mild interest and enjoyment in sex, slightly negative feelings about sex, or rejection of sexual relations. Table 1 presents the results on this

TABLE 1: *The Lower the Social Status, the Less Interest and Enjoyment Husbands and Wives Find in Marital Sexual Relations*

	Middle	Upper-Lower	Lower-Lower
Husbands			
Great interest and enjoyment	78%	75%	44%
Mild interest and enjoyment	22%	25%	56%
Number of cases	(56)	(56)	(59)
Wives			
Great interest and enjoyment	50%	53%	20%
Mild interest and enjoyment	36%	16%	26%
Slightly negative	11%	27%	34%
Reject sexual relations	3%	4%	20%
Number of cases	(58)	(68)	(69)

variable by social class. (Since there were no differences between the upper and lower portions of the middle class, these groups were combined in the tables.) It is apparent that as one moves from higher to lower social status the proportion of men and women who show strong interest and enjoyment of sex declines.

Among men the proportion showing only mild interest and enjoyment increases as one moves to the lower-lower class level. Among women the proportion who are slightly negative or rejecting in their attitudes toward sexual relations increases systematically from the middle to the upper-lower to the lower-lower class. (There is a small but consistent tendency for Negroes in the lower-lower class to show somewhat more interest in sex than similarly situated whites.) *

It would seem, then, that social status has a great deal to do with the extent to which couples manage in marriage to find sexual relations a valued and meaningful activity. This result is consistent with the findings of the Kinsey studies.[9, 14, 15] For women, the Kinsey study reports that erotic arousal from any source is less common at the lower educational levels, that fewer of these women have ever reached orgasm, and that the frequency for those who do is lower. For men, the pattern is less clear-cut as far as frequency goes, but it is apparent that fore-play techniques are less elaborate at the lower educational levels, most strikingly so with respect to oral techniques. In positional variations in intercourse, the lower educational levels show somewhat less versatility, but more interesting is the fact that the difference between lower and higher educational levels increases with age, because positional variations among lower status men drop away rapidly, while the decline among more educated men is much less. This same pattern characterizes nudity in marital coitus.

The lesser elaboration of the sexual relationship among lower class couples which this suggests is apparent in our qualitative data. The longer the lower class man is married, the

---

* It should be noted that the careful and detailed study of blue-collar marriages by Komarovsky[13] reports that there were no differences in sexual enjoyment between higher and lower status wives within the working class (status indicated by high school education or less than high school education). I have no explanation for this difference in findings between two studies which parallel each other in most other respects, but the readers should be aware of Komarovsky's contrary findings (see especially pp. 93–94). However, the less educated wives did view sex as more of a duty, and refused less often.

more likely he is to express a reduced interest in an enjoyment of sexual relations with his wife, as well as indicating reduced frequency of intercourse. In the middle class, while reduced frequency is universally recognized, there is much more of a tendency to put this in the context of "the quantity has gone down, but the quality gets better and better." An examination of the very small body of literature dealing with attitudes toward and feelings about sexual relations in lower class populations in other countries suggests that this pattern is not confined to the United States.[16, 19, 25, 26, 27]

Having observed that lower class husbands and wives are less likely than are middle class ones to find sexual relations gratifying, we become interested in why that should be. The major variable that seems related to this class difference concerns the quality of conjugal role relationships in the different classes. In this same study we found that middle class couples were much more likely to emphasize patterns of jointly organized activities around the home and joint activities outside the home, while working and lower class couples were much more likely to have patterns of role relationships in which there was greater emphasis on separate functioning and separate interests by husbands and wives. Following Bott[2] we have classified couples who show a fair degree of separateness in their conjugal role relationships as *highly segregated,* those who show a very strong degree of joint participation and joint involvement of each in the other's activities were characterized as *jointly organized.* Those couples who fall between these two extremes we have characterized as having *intermediate segregation* of conjugal role relationships. Very few working or lower class couples show the jointly organized pattern, but there is variation in the intermediate to the highly segregated range. When the influence of this variable on sexual enjoyment and interest is examined, we find a very strong relationship.

Table 2 indicates that it is primarily among couples in highly segregated conjugal role relationships that we find wives who reject or are somewhat negative towards sexual relations. Similarly, it is primarily among couples in less segregated conjugal role relationships that we find husbands and wives who express great interest and enjoyment in sexual relations.

These results suggest that the lower value placed on sexual relations by lower class wives, and to a lesser extent by lower class husbands, can be seen as an extension of the high degree of segregation in their conjugal role relationship more generally. The couple emphasize separateness in their other activities; therefore separateness comes to be the order of the day in their sexual relationship. Since the wife's interest in sex tends to be more heavily dependent upon a sense of interpersonal closeness and gratification in her total relationship with her husband, it is very difficult for her to find gratification in sex in the context of a highly segregated role relationship.

Close and gratifying sexual relationships are difficult to achieve because the husband and wife are not accustomed to

TABLE 2: *Lower Class Couples in Highly Segregated Conjugal Role Relationships Find Less Enjoyment in Sexual Relations*

	White Couples		Negro Couples	
	Inter-mediate Segre-gation*	Highly Segre-gated	Inter-mediate Segre-gation*	Highly Segre-gated
Husbands				
Great interest and enjoyment	72%	55%	90%	56%
Mild interest and enjoyment	28%	45%	10%	44%
Number of cases	(21)	(20)	(21)	(25)
Wives				
Great interest and enjoyment	64%	18%	64%	8%
Mild interest and enjoyment	4%	14%	14%	40%
Slightly negative	32%	36%	18%	32%
Reject sexual relations	—	32%	4%	20%
Number of cases	(25)	(22)	(22)	(25)

* Includes the few jointly-organized couples.

relating intimately to each other. It may well be that a close sexual relationship has no particular social function in such a system, since the role performances of husband and wife are organized on a separatist basis, and no great contribution is made by a relationship in which they might sharpen their ability for cooperation and mutual regulation. Examination of the six negative cases in our sample—that is, those in which despite a highly segregated role relationship the wife enjoys sex a great deal—indicates that this comes about when the wife is able to bring to the relationship her own highly autonomous interest in sex. To the extent that she is, on the other hand, dependent upon her husband for stimulation, encouragement, and understanding, she seems to find frustration in sex.

Husbands whose wives do not enjoy sexual relations are not particularly comfortable about this fact and in various ways either express some guilt, or try to conceal the state of affairs from both themselves and the interviewers. However, they seem to do little to correct the situation. Husbands in segregated relationships consistently overestimate the degree of gratification that their wives find in sex. Thus, half of the men in highly segregated relationships indicated that their wives enjoyed sex more than the wives themselves indicated, compared to only 21 per cent of the men in less segregated relationships.

Lower class men in highly segregated relationships seem to make few efforts to assist their wives in achieving sexual gratification, and place little emphasis on the importance of mutual gratification in coitus. For example, while 74 per cent of the lower and working class husbands with intermediate relationships give some spontaneous indication that they value mutual gratification in the sexual relationship, only 35 per cent of the husbands in segregated relationships speak of mutual gratification. It is not surprising, then, that a considerable number of wives complain about their husbands' lack of consideration. Forty per cent of the wives in segregated relationships spontaneously indicate that their husbands are inconsiderate of them in connection with sexual relations, compared to only

7 per cent of wives in intermediate relationships. Similarly, 38 per cent of those in highly segregated relationships spontaneously indicate that they consider sex primarily as a duty, compared to only 14 per cent of the wives in intermediate relationships.

These differences among classes, and within the lower class between couples in intermediate and highly segregated role relationships, continue to appear when the focus of inquiry is shifted from degree of enjoyment of sexual relations to the question of the psychosocial functions which people think sex serves for them. Two common themes stand out in the way couples talk about what sex "does" for men and women. One is that sex provides "psychophysiological" relief—it gets rid of tensions, relaxes, gives physical relief ("It's like the back pressure on a car that you have to get rid of."), and provides sensual pleasure in the form of orgasm. The other theme emphasizes, instead, the social-emotional gratifications that come from closeness with the partner, a growth of love, a sense of oneness, of sharing, of giving and receiving. Almost all of the respondents who mentioned one or the other of these functions mentioned the physical aspect, but there is quite a bit of variation in whether this is mentioned by itself or in combination with social-emotional closeness. Table 3 provides distributions by class and role relationship of the relative emphasis on these two themes.

The findings emphasize further the fact that one of the main differences between the middle class and the lower class, and within the lower class between couples in intermediate and highly segregated role relationships, has to do with the extent to which the sexual relationship is assimilated with other aspects of the on-going relationship between husband and wife. It seems very clear that in the middle class, and among those lower class couples with conjugal role relationships of intermediate segregation, the sexual relation is seen as an extension of an over-all husband-wife relationship which emphasizes "togetherness," mutual involvement, and give-and-take. In the lower class, among couples in highly segregated conjugal role

TABLE 3: *Lower Class Couples in Highly Segregated Conjugal Role Relationships See Only Psychophysiological Pleasure and Relief in Sexual Relations*

| | Middle Class | Lower Class | |
		Intermediate Segregation	Highly Segregated
Husbands			
Socioemotional closeness and exchange	75%	52%	16%
Psychophysiological pleasure and relief only	25%	48%	84%
Number of cases	(56)	(40)	(31)
Wives			
Socioemotional closeness and exchange	89%	73%	32%
Psychophysiological pleasure and relief only	11%	27%	68%
Number of cases	(46)	(33)	(22)

relationships, on the other hand, the sexual relationship is isolated from aspects of the husband-wife relationship and stands in sharp contrast to these other aspects because it requires concerted cooperation on the part of the two partners. Other data showed that in a great many cases, the wife's response is to cooperate only passively, by making herself available when her husband "wants it." In a few cases the wife is able to bring her own autonomous psychophysiological needs to sexual relations and find enjoyment in them.

LOWER CLASS NONMARITAL SEXUAL RELATIONS

We have much less systematic knowledge of lower class attitudes and customary behaviors concerning nonmarital sexual relations than for marital sexual relations. We do know, however, a fair amount about the incidence of nonmarital sexual relations from the Kinsey studies as this varies by social status (educational level). The considerable literature dealing with lower class adolescent peer groups also provides some insight into the place of premarital sexual relations in the peer group activities of young lower class boys and girls.

From the Kinsey studies of white males and females it seems clear that before the age of twenty both lower class boys and lower class girls are much more likely to have premarital coitus than are middle class boys and girls. However, even lower class girls are not as likely to have premarital sexual relations as are middle class boys; the overall cultural double standard seems to operate at all class levels. Further, after the age of twenty, status seems to influence premarital coitus in opposite ways for men and women. After that age middle class girls are more likely than lower class girls to have premarital relations, perhaps because the lower class girls are so quickly siphoned off into marriage, while lower class boys continue more frequently to have premarital relations.

From the Kinsey studies, we know that there are very great differences between white and Negro females in the extent to which they engage in premarital coitus. While the social class influence is the same in both groups, in the teens the level of exposure to sexual relations is on the order of three to four times higher for Negro girls than for white girls. Thus, while at age twenty only 26 per cent of white grammar school educated girls have had premarital sexual relationships, over 80 per cent of comparable Negro girls have.

These findings concerning premarital coitus are consistent with the impressions one gains from literature that deals with the peer group systems of white and Negro lower class adolescents and young adults.[3, 4, 8, 10, 11, 19, 21, 24, 29] In the white lower class there is a great deal of emphasis on the double standard in that white lower class boys are expected to engage in sexual relations whenever they have an opportunity and pride themselves on their ability to have intercourse with many different girls. "Making out" in this fashion is turned into valuable currency within the boys' peer groups; there is much bragging and competition (leading to not a little exaggeration) among white slum boys about their sexual conquests.

The girls' position in this group is a much more complex one. White slum groups tend to grade girls rather finely according to the extent of their promiscuity, with virgins being highly valued and often protected, "one man girls" still able to retain some respect from those around them (particularly if in the end they marry the boy with whom they have had intercourse), and more promiscuous girls quickly put into the category of an "easy lay." In groups, then, although boys are constantly exposed to stimulation to engage in sexual relations, efforts are made to protect girls from such stimulation and even to conceal from them elementary facts about sex and about their future sexual roles. Mothers do not discuss sex with their daughters, and usually do not even discuss menstruation with them. The daughter is left very much on her own with only emergency attention from the mother—for example, when she is unable to cope with the trauma of onset of menses or seems to be getting too involved with boys. When women at this level assess their premarital knowledge of sex, they generally say that they were completely unprepared for sexual relations in marriage or for their first premarital experiences, that no one had ever told them much about sex, and that they had only a vague idea of what was involved. There is little evidence that in this kind of white lower class subculture many girls find the idea of sexual relations particularly attractive. Although they may become involved with fantasies of romantic love, they seem to show little specific interest in sexual intercourse.

In the Negro lower class the clear-cut differences between the amount of sexual activity respectively permitted girls and boys (and men and women) that seem to obtain in the white lower class are absent. Indeed, at age fifteen, according to the Kinsey results, more grammar school educated Negro girls have experienced coitus than white boys; this is also true at the high school level. With over 60 per cent of grammar school educated Negro girls having had intercourse by the age of 15, and over 80 per cent by the age of twenty, it seems clear that with the Negro slum community, whatever the attitudes in-

volved, lower class Negro girls are introduced to sexual relations early and, relative to white girls, engage much more
frequently in sexual relations once they have started. There
are well-established patterns of seduction within Negro slum
communities which Negro boys employ. They are sharply
judged by other boys and girls on their ability to employ these
techniques, and boys show considerable anxiety lest they be
rated low on these skills. As is well known, this higher degree
of sexual activity leads to a high rate of illegitimacy.

These bare behavioral statistics might lead one to believe
that among the lower class Negroes, at least, there is a happy
acceptance of premarital sexual relations, somewhat along the
line of the natural-man myth discussed above. However, close
observation of ghetto peer group activities of late adolescent
and early adult Negro males and females indicates that such is
not the case.[4, 11] In the first place, attitudes toward sexual relations are highly competitive (among own sex peers), and
heavily exploitative (toward opposite sex). Slum Negro boys
typically refer to girls, including their own "girlfriends," as
"that bitch" or "that whore" when they talk among themselves. Negro girls who do engage in sexual relations in response to the strong lines of the boys who "rap to" them often
do not seem to find any particular gratification in sexual relations, but rather engage in sex as a test and symbol of their
maturity and their ability to be in the swim of things. Over
time, a certain proportion of these girls do develop their own
appreciation of sexual relations, and engage in them out of
desire as well as for extrinsic reasons. However, it seems clear
that the competitive and exploitative attitudes on both sides
make sexual relations a tense and uncertain matter as far as
gratification goes. In discussing marital sexuality we noted that
the high degree of conjugal role segregation seems to interfere
with achieving maximum gratification in sexual relations. A
parallel factor seems to operate in connection with premarital
relations. That is, because of the culturally defined and inter-
personally sustained hostilities that exist between the sexes, it
seems difficult for both boys and girls to develop a self-assured

and open acceptance of sex for the pleasure it can provide, much less for a heightened sense of interpersonal closeness and mutuality. When one seeks to study the meaning and function of sexual relations in such a very complex situation as the Negro lower class community, one becomes aware of how much more subtle and ramified the issues are than can be captured in the traditional categories of sex research.

THE FUTURE OF SEX IN THE LOWER CLASS

As the working class has attained greater prosperity and a sense of greater economic stability since World War II, there seems to have been a shift from traditional working class patterns of a high degree of conjugal role segregation and reliance by husbands and wives on their same sex peer groups for emotional support and counsel. Elsewhere Handel and Rainwater[12, 13] have discussed the increasing importance of a modern, working class life style which seems to be gradually replacing the traditional life style among those working class families who are in a position to partake of the "standard package" of material and social amenities which represent the common man's version of the "good American life." We have seen that among those couples who have a lesser degree of conjugal role segregation there is a much greater probability of a mutual strong interest in sexual relations and an emphasis on sexual relations as an extension of the socioemotional closeness that is valued in husband-wife relationships. We can predict, then, that shifts in the direction of greater cooperation and solidarity based on interpenetration of family role activities in marriage will carry with them an increased intimacy in the sexual sphere. This greater mutuality is both an expression of, and functional for, the increased self-sufficiency of a nuclear family, in which working class husband and wife now rely less on outsiders for support and a sense of primary group membership and more on each other. In this sense a "good" sexual relation between husband and wife can be seen as one of the major strengths of the adaptable nuclear family that Clark Vincent has argued is necessary for our kind of industrial society.[28]

But what of those members of the lower class who do not participate in the increasing prosperity and security that the great majority of the working class has known for the past twenty years? In recent years there has been mounting evidence that sex-related pathologies of the Negro slum ghetto community—for example, the rate of illegitimacy, venereal disease, drug-encouraged prostitution[4, 17]—are increasing rather than decreasing. It seems clear that so long as the socioeconomic circumstances of slum Negroes do not improve, we can expect only a worsening of a situation in which sexual relations are used for exploitative and competitive purposes. There is much less clear-cut evidence concerning white slum groups; it may well be that the rates for the same sex-related pathologies show lesser increases because the white poor are not confined to ghettos which serve to concentrate the destructive effects of poverty, but instead tend to be more widely dispersed in the interstices of more stable working class neighborhoods.[24]

In short, though we see some evidence to support the notion of a "sexual renaissance" with respect to marital sexuality in the modern working class, we see no such evidence with respect to the less prosperous lower class.

SEX RESEARCH IN THE LIGHT OF LOWER CLASS SEX BEHAVIOR

It is probably not unfair to say that efforts to study sexual behavior scientifically have been plagued by an obsessive preoccupation with the terms of the larger public dialogue on the subject, and with the value conflicts and contradictions evident in that dialogue. Thus, researchers who investigate sexual behavior have often been motivated by an effort to determine whether sex under particular circumstances is good or bad, or whether particular customs interfere with pleasure or are conducive to it. While these are legitimate concerns, they have tended to distract social scientists from an effort simply to understand sexual practices in their full human context. We have suggested that a close examination of lower class sexual behavior tends to disprove certain widely-held stereotypes—themselves not unknown in social scientists' own attitudes. But more important, the study of lower class sexual behavior emphasizes the importance of trying to understand such behavior both in the immediate context of relevant interpersonal relations (marital relations, peer group relations, and so forth) and in the context of the structural position of the actors, and the stresses and strains that position engenders. Such an understanding can only come about through careful empirical research that does not take for granted supposed "facts" about the actors involved but, rather, explores these interrelations empirically.

Once we have an adequate picture of the sexual behavior of individuals in a particular situation, we can begin to ask questions about the role of this sexual behavior in connection with other aspects of the individual's interpersonal relations. We can ask what the functions of particular forms of sexual behavior are for the individual and for the groups to which he belongs. More psychologically, we can ask, and not assume in advance that we know, what goals the individual seeks to effect through particular kinds of sexual behavior. It seems to me that this is the real legacy of Freud for the study of sexual behavior. Freud sought to show that sex is not simply sex, but a complex form of behavior built out of elements which extend genetically back into dim childhood history, and cross-sectionally into other vital interests which the individual seeks to maximize and protect. Just as any other applied field of social science profits from a wide application of contending theoretical paradigms, so the study of sexual behavior would profit from a more liberal application of the diverse conceptual tools at our disposal.

REFERENCES

1. Bordua, David J., "Delinquent Subcultures: Sociological Interpretations of Gang Delinquency." *The Annals of the American Academy of Political and Social Sciences,* 338 (1961), 120–36.
2. Bott, Elizabeth, *Family and Social Network* (London: Tavistock Publications, 1957).
3. Cayton, Horace R., and St. Clair Drake, *Black Metropolis* (New York: Harper & Row, 1962).
4. Clark, Kenneth, *The Dark Ghetto* (New York: Harper & Row, 1965).
5. Davis, Allison, *Social Class Influence on Learning* (Cambridge: Harvard University Press, 1952).
6. Dollard, John, *Caste and Class in a Southern Town* (New Haven: Yale University Press, 1937).
7. Erikson, Kai T., "Notes on the Sociology of Deviance." *Social Problems,* 9 (1962), 307–314.
8. Frazier, E. Franklin, *The Negro Family in the United States* (Chicago: University of Chicago Press, 1939).
9. Gebhard, Paul H., *et al., Pregnancy, Birth and Abortion* (New York: Harper & Row, 1958).
10. Green, Arnold W., "The Cult of Personality and Sexual Relations." *Psychiatry,* 4 (1941), 343–44.
11. Hammond, Boone, "The Contest System: A Survival Technique" (Master's Honors Essay Series; St. Louis, Mo.: Washington University, 1965).
12. Handel, Gerald, and Lee Rainwater, "Persistence and Change in Working Class Life Style," in Arthur B. Shostak and William Gomberg, eds., *Blue Collar Worlds* (Englewood Cliffs, N.J.: Prentice-Hall, 1964), pp. 36–42.
13. Komarovsky, Mirra, *Blue Collar Marriage* (New York: Random House, 1964).
14. Kinsey, Alfred C., *et al., Sexual Behavior in the Human Male* (Philadelphia: W. B. Saunders, 1948).
15. Kinsey, Alfred C., *et al., Sexual Behavior in the Human Female* (Philadelphia: W. B. Saunders, 1953).
16. Lewis, Oscar, *Life in a Mexican Village: Tepoztlán Restudied* (Urbana, Illinois: University of Illinois Press, 1951).
17. Moynihan, Daniel P., "Employment, Income and the Ordeal of the Negro Family," *Daedalus,* 94:4 (1965), 745–70.
18. Rainwater, Lee, *And The Poor Get Children* (Chicago: Quadrangle Books, 1960).
19. ———, "Marital Sexuality in Four Cultures of Poverty." *Journal of Marriage and the Family,* 26 (1964), 457–66.
20. ———, *Family Design: Marital Sexuality, Family Planning and Family Limitation* (Chicago: Aldine, 1965).
21. ———, "The Crucible of Identity: The Negro Lower Class Family." *Daedalus,* 95:1 (1966), 172–216.
22. Rainwater, Lee, Richard Coleman, and Gerald Handel, *Workingman's Wife: Her Personality, World and Life Style* (New York: Oceana Publications, 1959).

23. Rainwater, Lee, and Gerald Handel, "Changing Family Roles in the Working Class," in Arthur B. Shostak and William Gomberg, eds., *Blue Collar Worlds* (Englewood Cliffs, N.J.: Prentice Hall, 1964), pp. 70–76.

24. Short, J. F., and F. L. Strodtbeck, *Group Process and Gang Delinquency* (Chicago: University of Chicago Press, 1965).

25. Slater, Eliot, and Moya Woodside, *Patterns of Marriage* (London: Cassell, 1951).

26. Spinley, B. M., *The Deprived and the Privileged* (London: Routledge & Kegan Paul, 1953).

27. Stycos, J. Mayone, *Family and Fertility in Puerto Rico* (New York: Columbia University Press, 1955).

28. Vincent, Clark, "Familia Spongia: The Adaptive Function" (paper presented at the Annual Meeting of the National Council on Family Relations at Toronto, 1965).

29. Whyte, William F., "A Slum Sex Code," *American Journal of Sociology*, 49 (1943), 24–41.

7 : Social Class and the Psychiatric Patient: A Study in Composite Character

ALAN L. GREY

An unpleasant truth confronting the mental health professions is that psychotherapeutic care of the poor is markedly inadequate. In a major study of this problem, which found significantly higher incidence and prevalence of psychoses at the lowest socioeconomic level in New Haven, it is tersely put that the lowest socioeconomic stratum "needs help most—social and psychiatric—and gets it least."[13] The difficulty lies not merely in the inability of the underprivileged to pay for treatment or obtain it free of cost. Even more disturbing is the apparent ineffectiveness of such treatment once it has been secured. According to the findings of another large scale research, "Within the universe of patient-therapist relationships,

This chapter is a condensed version of an article that originally appeared in the William Alanson White Institute publication, *Contemporary Psychoanalysis*, 2 (1966), 87–121. It is reprinted here with the permission of the publishers.

the chances of a successful outcome . . . seem to vary considerably among the several socioeconomic segments of the patient population in a range from about seven in ten of the top segment to three in ten of the bottom one."[84] A successful outcome was defined here in terms of social functioning as rated independently by two psychiatrists.[34]

THE BACKGROUND OF THE PROBLEM

What is the source of the trouble? The answer most often given by experts involved in working with the lower class patient population is, "the middle class character of the mental health movement and the associated inappropriate nature of the services offered to low income people."[32] New departures in treatment designed to suit the needs of the poor are the solutions they propose. Another widespread view whose blunt expression sometimes finds its way into print holds that, since the poor seem incapable of benefiting from psychotherapy, we systematically confine this mode of treatment to the higher social levels.[15]

A number of questions are intertwined in the various ongoing controversies.

Are lower class patients actually given less extensive psychiatric care, even when all financial barriers are removed? If so, is it due primarily to their lesser importance in the eyes of middle class therapists?

Or is there evidence of other factors, such as a tendency among lower class patients to be less responsive to customary treatment procedures because of different personality orientation?

If such a distinction exists between lower class and middle class patients, does it center essentially around discrepant value systems, or do other significant aspects of personality vary predictably from one status level to another?

These issues are of sufficient importance, socially and theoretically, to merit careful examination of the available evidence. Hollingshead and Redlich, for example, offer striking indications of class differences based on their New Haven patient census, but at the same time acknowledge a pressing need for further data to determine which of their various observations will hold for equivalent patient status groups in other parts of the United States. Systematic clinical evidence must ". . . appear in other samples and in other areas of behavior before the existence of classes as functional status groups can be said to be demonstrated."[13]

One aspect of this paper is the presentation of a study of relationships between social class and personality characterizing patients in a midwestern mental hospital. These results will be compared with published reports about other patient groups and also about nonpatient populations. The comparison with "normal" samples is an additional test of class-character generalizations suggested by psychoanalytic theory, which by and large held that the abnormal is continuous with the normal. Thus, meaningful relationships between class and character occurring in patients should also be detectable in the general population. Seen in this context of related studies, our data will help to assess whether the status concept is of theoretical and practical use to the psychoanalyst.

THE BACKGROUND OF THE RESEARCH PROGRAM: SOCIAL CLASS AND ITS INTERCONNECTIONS WITH CHARACTER

Experts adopt somewhat varying classificatory systems, depending partly on the nature of the group studied and partly on their purposes. Warner's approach,[39, 40] summarized here, was the method employed for this study because the schemes of Hollingshead, Srole, and others essentially derive from it.

The Warner group devised a scale which assigns a numerical score to each of the following seven prestige-related characteristics: occupation, source of income (inherited, earned, and so on), house type, dwelling area, education, amount of income, ethnic origin. From these is derived an Index of Social Characteristics (ISC), whose numerical score places the rated subject in an appropriate category.

In our own study sample, half of the patients were identified as middle class and the other half as lower class. Each major class in turn was subdivided into an upper and lower subgroup. The initials used for convenience in designating each status category in this study (and in the sociological literature) and representative associated occupations are as follows:

MC—*Middle Class*
UMC—Upper-Middle Class: lawyer, factory manager
LMC—Lower-Middle Class: salesman, office worker
LC—*Lower Class*
ULC—Upper-Lower Class: barber, semi-skilled worker
LLC—Lower-Lower Class: laborer, tenant farmer

Utilizing Fromm's position, three hypotheses for testing and comparison were derived relevant to the interconnections between social class, social character, and psychotherapy.

1. MC mental health personnel regard and treat MC patients more favorably than they do LC patients.

2. The *observed* behavior (for example, a facet of "social character") of MC patients is more consonant with expectations of MC hospital staff than is LC patient behavior.

3. There are significant differences between MC and LC patients in their recalled experiences as children and as adults. (For these other aspects of social character, inquiry is focused primarily on family life.)

THE SAMPLE

The research program was conducted in 1949, before the current burgeoning of interest in psychotherapy with the poor. (A detailed report of results is available on microfilm only.[9])

The sample of forty male patients, divided equally between MC and LC, was observed and intensively interviewed at a Veterans Administration psychiatric hospital near a large urban area in the Middle West. The sample size is small in terms of the magnitude of the total population to which it belongs, but fairly large by comparison with subsequent research of a similarly intensive nature. In the case study aspect of Hollingshead and Redlich's New Haven project, for example, there was a total of twenty-five males.[26] Because samples in this field have been small and because the patient universe in the United States is large, it becomes important to cross-check consistency of results in different geographic areas.

Subjects in our sample were selected from the "Convalescent Section" of the hospital, actually a group of wards for legally competent patients, including recent admissions, who were not expected to require long-term institutionalization. Patients were free to terminate their hospital stay at any time and encouraged to leave for intervals up to several days while still officially registered at the installation. This policy attracted a somewhat larger proportion of MC veterans than was usually found in free institutions. The criteria for admission to these wards imposed a functional rather than diagnostic emphasis. This yardstick eliminated those most severely disturbed who would be incapable of informative interviews and in whose cases the question of constitutional factors arose more urgently.

The study sample was composed, then, of legally competent psychiatric patents, all of whom had been in military service during World War II. They all were at least third generation gentile Americans with no conspicuous ethnic features in their background. The term "ethnic" here is used to designate distinctly recognizable foreign cultural characteristics such as the regular use of a foreign language in the home, residence in a foreign nationality neighborhood, or attendance of a recognizably foreign church. All subjects were reared by their own families, all of which included a natural, or legal, father and mother. Since ethnic backgrounds and broken homes[33] are more frequent in the lower class, and since the influence of these factors might be attributed spuriously to the status difference itself, the control of such variables provides an unusually rigorous test of social class influence. In determining class level, Warner's Index of Social Characteristics was used to estimate the status of the patient's father during that patient's first twelve years of life, spent in what sociologists have termed his "family of orientation" or childhood family. Orientation status is more pertinent to this study than is current status, since the childhood milieu is an important focus of interest for us.

Patients were selected for the sample on the simple basis of "first come, first served," provided that they fulfilled the sociological criteria described above. This procedure proved very satisfactory, for several later comparisons of the study sample with total Convalescent Section population indicated no "significant" differences between them. Our criteria for "significance" were statistical (that is, a minimal confidence limit of .05), and all findings to be reported were "significant" in this statistical sense unless otherwise noted.

The average subject was about thirty years old, psychoneurotic (72 per cent), either single or parted from his wife (67 per cent), and Protestant (63 per cent). Once chosen for the study, he was interviewed by either of two clinical psychologists for three or four sessions totaling from eight to twelve hours. Afterward, supplementary data were gathered from his responses to written questionnaires, from hospital records, and from interviews with hospital staff members who had worked with him.

HYPOTHESIS 1: HOW HOSPITAL STAFF REGARDS AND TREATS PATIENTS OF TWO SOCIAL CLASSES

Moving from method to content, the first issue for investigation concerns the professional staff of the hospital and how well their responses to patients can be predicted simply from information about the patients' social status. The problem is advisedly stated, at this point, as one of prediction alone. That is, the first step simply is to establish whether there are differences between the two class groups in the clinical evaluations and amount of treatment accorded them. The exploration of underlying causes is best done step by step and is undertaken, insofar as our data allow, in subsequent sections of this study. Without specific evidence it is unwarranted to assume that any observed differences are due to prejudice.

Do empirical results show differences? Briefly, LC patients are less often given psychotherapy and, when given, it involves fewer contacts and results in less improvement as judged by hospital staff. As members of the general patient community, LC men are seen as less acceptable by hospital administration, an evaluation they reciprocate by removing themselves more rapidly from it when permitted to do so. All of these data support Hypothesis 1, that "MC mental health personnel regard and treat MC patients more favorably than they do LC patients."

Hypothesis 2: Social Class and Patient Behavior

Closer examination of class-related differences in patient behavior may illuminate the nature of the trouble between LC patients and staff. The investigation can begin with the fact that LC patients committed more major infractions of hospital rules and more "AWOLS." Serious infractions of rules usually involved such matters as bringing liquor onto hospital premises, returning from leave in a disruptively intoxicated state, repeated overstay of leave without notification, and neglect or defiance of regulations for the maintenance of cleanliness and order on the wards. This LC lack of discipline was also reflected in less flamboyant acts, related in spirit and coalescing into a fairly consistent picture.

These lesser infractions might be illustrated by looking at a time-honored behavior clue used in psychotherapy—promptness and reliability in attendance. In itself, tardiness or absence becomes important only when it seriously reduces the time available for treatment. Some of the significance of irregularity, too, lies in its correlation with other manifestations of resistance not so easily accounted for in statistical testing. Even when he does appear for meetings, the irregular patient is often less communicative and generally less motivated toward a therapeutic objective. These ramifications are reinforced by the high value placed on promptness in middle class American culture. Even if the patient's own social background does not accord a similar high value to time regularity, he gives an impression to the middle class clinician of lack of concern about the therapeutic enterprise.

Were the MC patients more reliable about appointments? Records kept by hospital vocational advisors indicated that half of those MC's who consulted them were "very regular" in attendance, and that this was true for *none* of the LC's. The records of the psychologist-therapists similarly show that none of their MC patients missed as many as a fifth of scheduled meetings, but that almost half (46 per cent) of the LC sampling exceeded this amount. Not only in his repudiation of hospital rules, then, but also in his responses to treatment services when they are proffered, the LC patient shows a well-defined pattern of noncompliance with the expectations of hospital authorities and their psychotherapeutic methods.

Previously published studies have shown that LC patients avail themselves less of psychiatric *outpatient* treatment even when cost is not a barrier.[2] This has sometimes been attributed to the general lack of information or greater fear of hospitals in the lower class. Our results underscore that even after the LC patient is hospitalized, after there has been hospital exposure to "mental health education" meetings, with maximum physical accessibility to the professional office and explicit reminders by the nursing staff, he continues to be reluctant. These observations coincide sufficiently with other reports to warrant the conclusion that we are witnessing a general estrangement between professionals and their LC patients, rather than the shortcomings of a particular institution. Moreover, some of the reasons for this apparent lack of success with LC patients seem to lie deeper than those involving accessibility of information, hospitalization fears, and the like.

Having seen the limitations of circumstantial explanations, we must now consider those hypotheses having graver implications. The most widely known of these hypotheses is that the difficulty lies in class prejudice on the part of the professional worker.

As a safeguard against unwarranted assumptions, certain questions merit serious considerations: Do LC patients display a pattern of antagonism and discipline only in response to the values of the therapist and other middle class people? Or do they have a generally different orientation toward authority, of whatever class, than do MC patients? If so, is this LC authority orientation integral to an even more extensive patterning of LC personality, to a LC social character distinguishably different from the MC orientation? If such class-character differences are observable, how compatible are current psychotherapeutic techniques with identifiable potentialities of the LC social character for learning and change? Even tentative answers to these questions may help in a fuller assessment of causes and remedies.

Beginning with reactions to authority, case histories may be examined to assess whether LC patients typically break the rules more often than MC's, as they were observed to do in the hospital. LC autobiographical recollections are more indicative of this tendency than are MC reports. For instance, drinking, gambling, and nonmarital sex activities began earlier and, with certain qualifications, continue to be a more regular part of their lives, as are physical battles with peers. More LC patients had been arrested for breaking the law in various ways (45 per cent LC and 15 per cent MC). It is difficult to find a precise analogue in extra-hospital behavior to being AWOL, but significantly more of our LC patients had run away from their parents' homes as children (80 per cent LC and 27 per cent MC) and had played hookey from school (85 per cent LC and 60 per cent MC). The LC pattern of "acting out against society, their family, and themselves"[20] has also been noted in other studies of psychiatric patients.

For certain of these behavior patterns we need not confine ourselves to patient populations but can compare the lower class way of life with the middle class in the general or "normal" population. Turning to the context of "total institution" other than the mental hospital—i.e., the armed forces—we have the finding of Stouffer and his associates[29] that World War II soldiers who had not completed high school (a crude index of LC status) wound up in the guardhouse for AWOL offenses significantly more often than those soldiers with more education. Similar knowledge about higher crime rates among the less educated in the civilian community has been available to sociologists for some time.[23]

Such information demonstrates that "acting out" against authority is not a response aimed at the middle class therapist and his class-limited experience and values. The traditionally lower class milieu of the Army and of urban tenement neighborhoods evoke similar responses from LC men. It is an LC style of reaction in many social contexts, even in nonpatient LC populations. Evidence from the general sociological literature as well as our own, then, supports the second hypothesis, that there are observable behavioral differences on a class basis.

Particularly significant, this hypothesis suggests that the psychotherapist is not necessarily the active instigator of his LC patient's antagonism and flight, but rather, that such behavior reflects the inadequate state of present knowledge about coping with readily aroused LC patient defenses. The implication here is that the development of remedies for the treatment impasse requires the consideration of more than differences in values. The therapist is to a large extent impeded by inertia—not an exclusively middle class vice—that comes from the reluctance of any highly trained person to relinquish familiar skills and the feeling of expertise in favor of uncertain experimentation. A further impediment to the therapeutic effectiveness is a lack of sophistication in psychosocial concepts. This partly reflects an oversight in training in all of the mental health professions—a neglect to teach relevant information already known about the larger social context in which both patient and therapist live. And part of what is not taught simply is not known. Cross-cultural adaptation of psychotherapy is currently at one of the boundaries of knowledge in this field. Awareness of the deficiencies may help to dispel the inertia.

An unfortunate hazard in relating to someone from another subculture who speaks one's own language is that one may misinterpret his life circumstances, his style of communication, or his social role, without even realizing it. The therapist may be particularly puzzled by the seeming paradox of impulsivity and acting out of feelings as inferred from the history of an LC patient and the picture of restraint and deference which is presented in the consulting room. To reduce confusion with LC patients, it may be useful to draw a sharp distinction between "impulsivity" and autonomy, or freedom from conventionality. As expressed by Fenichel:". . . there is a tendency to equate 'socially low' and 'instinctually uninhibited,' and 'socially high' and 'sublimated,' 'inhibited.' "[6] "Psychodynamic" thinking may even reinforce such confusion if it loosely equates "direct expression of instincts" of sexuality and aggression with spontaneous behavior, lack of inhibition.

Considering LC men in the light of our sociological information, it is clear that even their "swift action without forethought," as impulsivity has been defined,[12] may be decreed culturally for given circumstances. Thus, the prescribed and inculcated masculine role in the lower class may call for defiant behavior as the appropriate style for coping with lost or hurt feelings. In the LC milieu, aggressive acts may be the way to avert particular dangers associated with crying, pleading, talking things over, or even letting oneself or anyone else know of such inclinations. Insofar as being "natural" implies direct expression or communication of inner feeling, the LC man's "impulsive" act of defiance is hardly that. Is it not a concealment, a failure in self-expression, an abdication of personal autonomy to social convention? Such defensive patterns can be so strongly reinforced by experience, and alternative skills of direct verbal communication may be so atrophied, as to create a barrier unbreachable by communication techniques adequate in a different subculture.

Case literature is replete with examples of apparent misunderstandings by clinicians who regard the lower class as "less conforming" when in fact it may be that the patient, rather than conforming to the therapist's customs, follows *his own* LC norms rather rigidly. This image of LC man as nonconformist is held even by social class experts in the mental health field.[26] Which is the case for our lower class sample? Can it be said that they are, as a group, more spontaneous or more rigid in their personal relationships than MC patients? The question brings us to our third and last hypothesis, which investigates intrafamilial experiences.

HYPOTHESIS 3: CLASS DIFFERENCES IN RECALLED INTRAFAMILIAL EXPERIENCES

The patients in our sample grew up during those years before World War II that were clouded by economic depression. Almost half of the LC group (40 per cent) recalled their families as having received public assistance during that time but, as might be expected, there was only one such respondent in the MC group. Food donations, hand-me-down clothing, and all the other unpleasant accompaniments of poverty were considerably more frequent in the childhood experiences of LC patients.

Beyond that, the information at our disposal suggests the following picture: During childhood, LC training emphasizes response to externally imposed regulations: ". . . the blue-collar parents have retained a pre-Freudian innocence about human behavior. . . . If they puzzle over the rebelliousness or obedience of their children, they seek the explanation in discipline and wonder if they have been 'too easy.' . . ."[20] Compared with MC training, the LC family demonstrates a relative neglect of those parental techniques likely to induce internalized, self-regulatory restraints. The parent, notably the father, is less closely involved in his son's life than is the case in the MC home, whether it be to share pleasures, provide direction, or set consistent disciplinary limits. The LC boy does not find or expect much empathic response from parental or other authorities. Encountering difficulties with people or circumstances, he is likely to interpret them, as his own problem behavior was understood by his parents, as due to the recalcitrance of hostile forces. This externalizing orientation is likely to be reinforced by experience with agents of the larger community, teachers and police, for instance, who are more impatient with him, more likely to antagonize, than if he were a "nice middle class boy."

Experiences outside the home also tend to expose the LC father's limitations in both commanding respect from even minor figures of authority in the community, as well as his lack of power to act in the boy's behalf. Father becomes progressively less attractive and is depicted in his son's interviews as neither effectively helpful nor responsive. In fact, *most* authorities are assumed to be unresponsive. The powerful ones, such as community figures, and the father, as experienced in early childhood, are found to be basically harsh or indifferent. Additionally, the father later emerges as often ineffectual—a situation which is especially distressing to the boy whose implicit frame of reference "solves" difficulties by reliance on external agencies. Seen in the context of the treatment situation, this pattern of conflicts lends itself to a characteristic transference reaction in which the LC patient longs for a strong protector but is impelled to fight against the need in himself by repudiating the therapist in order to defend against the pain of anticipated disappointment.

Miller has pointed out the ". . . lack of a consistently present male figure with whom to identify and from whom to learn essential components of a male role." He adds that since ". . . women serve as a primary object of identification during preadolescent years, the almost obsessive lower class concern with 'masculinity' probably resembles a type of compulsive 'reaction-formation.' "[25] Our own psychotherapeutic activities with the LC patient do indicate a tendency to build up a self-protective veneer of toughness to reinforce his uncertain masculine identification, to deny his need for male authority figures who, according to his own past experience, are likely to prove untrustworthy. As Fenichel succinctly says about certain "acting-out" patients, "Their impulsive acts may then signify a striving for a goal which they simultaneously try to avoid because they are afraid of it."[6]

Such a formulation not only accounts for the observed LC wariness toward psychotherapy relationships, but suggests possible remedies. For instance, a well-conceived authoritarian treatment style might engage members of this social stratum more successfully than the classic rule that ". . . the analyst divorces himself as completely as possible from direct control of the patient's life."[21] This time-honored principle of detachment may be recognized as implicitly geared to the internalizing personality orientation of the middle class. While "the rule" is often violated in practice, the proposal that it be abandoned in principle with a certain social group may be sufficiently disturbing to some readers (to call their attention to the kinds of value conflicts that can involve the therapist working with LC populations). At any rate, the intervention tactic is suggested here, not as the writer's value preference, but simply in connection with his prediction that it would reduce the number of blue-collar dropouts at clinics. The prediction apparently is confirmed by such evidence as the following:

> Analysis of findings from Charles Kadushin's unpublished study of the attitudes toward psychotherapy of 1,400 applicants for treatment at hospitals and clinics in New York City, 1962. It was found that lower socioeconomic individuals who locate their problems environmentally prefer that psychotherapy be highly directive. This was far less true for the lower socioeconomic group who viewed the cause of their difficulties in somatic terms.[30]

This does not constitute a recommendation for the routine use of authoritarian techniques with the poor. In all clinical work, the particular patient must be appraised individually and procedures adjusted accordingly. The point is that insofar as the LC patient fits this composite portrait, the psychoanalytically trained therapist may function more effectively if he is free enough to reconsider approaches heretofore discouraged by dictums of his professional ideology.

Orientations to Intimacy

Obstacles to psychotherapy with LC patients arise not only from reluctance of the therapist to take a strong directive position. Both therapist and LC patient may find themselves baffled by certain divergent value orientations in each other that never emerge into explicit language. The MC therapist, for example, sets great store by empathic capacity, the ability to share intimate feeling, as both a private and a professional virtue. Despite whatever limitations he may have in this quality, his MC patient usually accords it a similarly high place; in fact, greater empathic experience may be his major treatment goal. The widely observed American need for "love"[8] is peculiarly true of the MC American. To the LC male patient, the phenomenon—as an aware experience mediated by words—is usually unimportant and difficult to understand. The impediments posed to introspective "insight" treatment by this externalizing tendency are formidable.

The experience of interviewing our sample presented many qualitative indications of this nonintrospective orientation in the lower class. A most conspicuous indicator—assuming the interviewee to be a willing informant—lies in the absence of certain kinds of statements, in a poverty of sensitive psychological reactions to significant people. "Sensitivity" here denotes not accuracy or perceptiveness, but awareness and concern about subjective experiences. For instance, when LC patients were asked to reminisce about their parental homes, even with specific questioning, a substantial proportion of them could recall no differences between their parents in attitudes toward relatives and friends (30 per cent LC and 5 per cent MC), did not remember whether their father or mother had any favorites among the children (55 per cent LC and 25 per cent MC), forgot whether the children ever had been compared with each other (65 per cent LC and 25 per cent MC), and also affirmed that they were unconcerned about such matters (40 per cent LC and 11 per cent MC). But rather than multiply such illustrations, one can see more directly the ramifications of this tendency by assessing their effect on the task of the psychotherapist. A tally of reports by treating psychologists who worked with members of our study sample indicates that while *all* MC patients spontaneously spoke of problems involving family ties and dependency feelings, only about half (56 per cent) of the LC group did so. Considering its conspicuousness in the clinical setting, one is hardly surprised to encounter references to it in a number of publications.[10, 31]

The LC tendency to perceive events, even human relationships, primarily in terms of the external and the tangible is well described by Komarovsky in an account of her interviews with nonpatient "blue-collar" wives:

> For me perhaps the most surprising aspect of the blue-collar world had to do not with manners and morals, but with the cognitive style of the people. . . . The word "surprise" was usually taken to mean an unexpected present. The word "help" meant money or services, not help in the psychological sense. "When you feel that way [low for no apparent reason] can your mother help you?" The woman might pause for a moment, being puzzled by the *non sequitur,* and say, "No, she doesn't have any cash to spare."[20]

LC lack of verbal contact with subjective feelings was quite consistent, ranging over a wide sampling of personal relationships. Whether it was early family history or current friendship, whether it involved male friends or wives or sweethearts, the same absence of reference to emotion, to intimacy, was evident. When asked to talk about any dissatisfactions with their closest buddy, most LC patients (61 per cent) could find nothing wrong with him, but most MC's (80 per cent) did identify dislikes. This was not simply because MC's felt more negatively about their friends. In fact, significantly more MC men made explicit references to the intimacy and duration of their relationships (60 per cent MC and 25 per cent LC). In the socially highest subgroups (UMC), most men also spoke of consulting their friends for personal advice (56 per cent UMC and 19 per cent of all others). Class predispositions toward seeking help from male authorities, including fathers and therapists, are pointedly suggested by these data.

Class differences are also reflected from the very outset of heterosexual activity for our sample. Significantly more LC patients recalled their early dating history as enjoyable (80 per cent LC and 50 per cent MC), and more frequently had sexual relationships with girls who were their social peers (45 per cent LC and 20 per cent MC). Do lower class men more readily establish close and spontaneous relationships with women, or does their greater ease with them derive from different, perhaps less demanding, goals? A significantly higher divorce rate in the lower class, generally, argues against the idea of happier LC relationships with women, but still leaves the matter obscure.

To clarify the quality of their heterosexual relationships, patients were interviewed about many matters, including what they sought in marriage. MC's were considerably more inclined to express a desire for emotional intimacy and support (79 per cent MC and 42 per cent LC), for a woman who would offer affection and understanding (75 per cent MC and 50 per cent LC). All MC's felt they should and would speak of almost anything with this wife, but about a quarter of the LC's (28 per cent) had important reservations about discussing even their own mutual sexual relations. If LC men are rather reserved, the MC's reveal an undiscriminating belief in the discussion of "everything." This MC overstress on intimacy serves as a reminder that the higher status patients are not without their own problems, although our focus on LC characteristics may distract inadvertently from that obvious fact.

MC concern about wifely companionship was also revealed in the definite ideas most of them (90 per cent MC) had formulated about how much education their mates should have, while this was stated as a matter of little or no importance to many LC subjects (45 per cent). It was not that MC patients wanted maximally educated spouses but rather that, in their more egalitarian conception of relations between the sexes, they consciously sought women whose educational backgrounds would not be too far from their own level in either direction. In fact, a quarter of the MC's spontaneously observed that "too much" education might lead a wife to regard herself as the man's superior. Worries of this sort did not trouble any LC's whose conscious views were predicated unquestioningly on the traditional formula of male superiority. This difference between classes in sex roles is depicted another way in a recent study of LC marriage in a nonpatient population:

> For working class couples there is no issue over who does what around the house. Not only the men, but even the women, accept the traditional division of masculine and feminine tasks, and the women do not expect assistance from their husbands in every day circumstances. Moreover, whereas educated women have misgivings about being "just a housewife," not a trace of this attitude appears in the blue-collar class.[20]

The contrast between LC conventionalization of male-female relationships, and MC personalization of them, is depicted nowhere more clearly than in sexual matters. This may appear surprising in the light of LC "impulsive" tendencies, but again it urges a distinction between impulsivity, which may be culturally stereotyped, and spontaneity. LC conventionality in sexual matters is quite consistent, in fact, with an overall view of LC male behavior as a stylized masculinity, a defensive separateness from women arising from uncertainty about one's role identification and mastery. As to the evidence itself, significantly more MC patients practiced variations in sexual intercourse beyond the conventional act. More MC patients held the view that "anything goes" which is acceptable to both partners and not injurious physically. It was clear, too, that the MC's spoke more freely with their sex partners about their mutual sex experience and consequently were more aware of the partners' reactions and preferences.

Once again, data about the nonpatient population coincides with our own. In this case, it is the extensive work of the Kinsey group.[17]

Another report on sexual attitudes also becomes relevant here: Else Frenkel-Brunswik observes about the authoritarian-minded that their values in sexual matters ". . . tend to be *conventionally determined* as opposed to the more *individualized* values of low scoring subjects"[1] and again, that "A lack of individuation and of real object relationship can be found in the field of sex as it was previously found in the attitude toward the parents (author's italics)."

The authoritarian character syndrome is a pattern of responding in human relationships, marked by a hierarchical rather than egalitarian inclination, close adherence to conventionally determined acts and beliefs, avoidance of intimacy, externalization of blame, and "acting out" behavior. Because of the coincidence of tendencies in our LC patient sample with this construct, it becomes meaningful to speak of a *lower class authoritarian character orientation*, which is significantly more frequent in that stratum than among MC patients.

While there is no implication that this pattern is identical with the authoritarianism of another class, culture, or time, or that it describes all lower class patients, the evidence of several studies suggests that it has practical diagnostic utility. It can help to predict behavior and provide clues to treatment approaches, as will be amplified in the following pages. Moreover, it is in accordance with the psychoanalytic principle which holds that the abnormal is continuous with the normal, and with actual data of other cited tendencies in the general, nonpatient population. In short, the presented evidence supports our third hypothesis, that there are significant differences between MC and LC male patient groups in terms of recalled interpersonal experiences as children and as adults in the specific areas of inquiry.

The following summary of all results will facilitate the further consideration of implications.

SUMMARY OF FINDINGS

1. Middle class personnel of a psychiatric hospital were found to regard and treat middle class (male) patients more favorably than lower class (male) patients. They judged the outcome of treatment to be more favorable for middle class patients.

2. The observed hospital behavior of middle class (male) patients differed significantly in certain respects from that of their lower class counterparts. Specifically, the higher status group observed hospital procedures more carefully and engaged significantly less in acting out behavior.

3. There were significant differences between the two social class levels in their reports of certain childhood experience and current relationships.

A. As adults, lower class patients are significantly more inclined than their middle class fellows to regard and respond to others in a conventionally determined fashion. They manifest less desire for intimacy, more "acting out" behavior in the community, and other tendencies that might be summarized as a "lower class authoritarian orientation."

B. A connection was suggested between this lower class character pattern and certain factors in the lower class "composite case history." Factors which are significantly more prominent in the LC childhood history are: less parental help and attention, a more authoritarian disciplinary climate, and a less favorable basis for positive identification with the father. Resulting uncertainty about one's masculine role may be particularly relevant in the development of authoritarian tendencies.

IMPLICATIONS FOR PSYCHOANALYSIS

What does this imply for psychoanalysis as a treatment method? The answer calls for several predictions, including a guess about how analysts will choose to define their methods and spheres of operation in the future. Maintained in its present form, psychoanalysis can persist as the intensive psychotherapy of the middle classes and of those from other classes who meet its characterological specifications. Conceived very broadly, to include all procedures designed to reintegrate dissociated aspects of the psyche, the problem of extending the scope of psychotherapy to benefit LC patients should be one which permits of a solution. Such work could lead to important expansions in conceptions and techniques, comparable to the "character analysis" revolution of several decades ago.

The nature of those new techniques can only be surmised from a survey of methods already proposed for work with the LC. One recent publication[29] advocates approaches which rely less on introspection and encourage "motoric activities" suitable to the LC personality style. Also favored are procedures that make problems immediate and concrete and therefore presumably more involving for the LC patient. Role-playing[31] is recommended, as are family therapy, group therapy, and the "multiple intervention" of the case work tradition. "Pills and needles" are suggested by these same authors as supplementary devices to satisfy LC needs for magic and authority. As a guiding principle, one paper asserts:

> It has been found that with blue-collar workers and lower socio-economic groups it is more practical to set direct and immediate treatment goals . . . rather than gear treatment toward long-range personality reorganization.[10]

Do the limited treatment goals urged for LC patients imply that this group is more severely damaged, or only that it seeks less? Unhappily, there is a lack of measuring devices for clear-cut determination of severity of illness. Epidemiological studies reveal a higher per capita rate of LC patients in hospitals, but this greater prevalence may be indicative of an accumulation due to neglect rather than a higher incidence of breakdown. Another factor complicating evaluation of degree of illness among the poor is a kind of partisan loyalty frequently observed among the experts. For example:

> Considering the lack of opportunities and difficult life conditions of the worker, a lower class psychodiagnostic record which is identical with that of a middle class person might be presumed to indicate greater health and better prognosis.[29]

The middle class humanistic tradition of loyalty to the underdog and reservations about the bourgeoisie shines through this statement like a beacon. Meritorious in themselves, such sentiments may breed impatience with facts and ultimately lead to unrealistic policies. Thus, recent social commentary is richly garnished with references to "white collar alienation" while, ironically, class-character research indicates that unawareness of feeling and avoidance of intimacy are significantly more extensive in lower class groups. Moreover, the pragmatic yardstick of treatment results suggests greater difficulty in achieving characterological change in LC patients, a limitation accepted even by experts developing improved methods.

Disregard of these facts may not prove a service to the LC patient in the long run, because it may lead unwittingly to overestimation of what treatment alone can accomplish for them. A more tempered enthusiasm might propose that, *in addition to treatment*, other strategies be considered in work with the lower class. If more difficult life situations can be expected to generate more severe emotional disturbance, then "closely linked with economic under-privilege is psychological under-privilege"[18] and careful consideration should be given to preventive measures. Programs should be designed to identify and modify social conditions which actively intensify the stresses of lower class life. This calls for a new kind of mental health expert, equipped to assess the psychological impact of the larger socio-political processes on the individual. The degree to which these factors influence emotional health should not be minimized. As a more immediate goal, serious attention should be given to the development and use of preventive psychotherapeutic techniques during preschool and early school years with children who live in areas showing high mental illness rates. These children need to be reached before barriers to certain aspects of human relationship have become so fixed as to interfere profoundly with availability to emotional contact in daily life or in psychological treatment.

REFERENCES

1. Adorno, T. W., Else Frenkel-Brunswik, D. J. Levinson, and R. N. Sanford, *The Authoritarian Personality* (New York: John Wiley, 1964), pp. 267–268, 402–404.
2. Avnet, Helen H., *Psychiatric Insurance* (New York: Group Health Insurance, Inc., 1962), pp. 36–87.
3. Brill, N. Q., and H. Storrow, "Social Class and Psychiatric Treatment," *Arch. Gen. Psychiat.*, 3:10 (1963), 340–344.
4. Clausen, J. A., *Sociology and the Field of Mental Health* (New York: Russell Sage Foundation, 1956).
5. Erikson, E. H., *Childhood and Society* (New York: W. W. Norton, 1950), p. 371.
6. Fenichel, O., *The Psychoanalytic Theory of Neurosis* (New York: W. W. Norton, 1945), pp. 96, 368.
7. Fromm, E., *Escape from Freedom* (New York: Holt, Rinehart & Winston, 1941), pp. 277–280.
8. Gorer, G., *The American People: A Study in National Character* (New York: W. W. Norton, 1948), chapt. 4.
9. Grey, A., "Relationship between Social Status and Psychiatric Characteristics of Psychiatric Patients" (Unpublished doctoral dissertation, University of Chicago, 1949).
10. Gurin, G., J. Veroff, and Sheila Feld, *Americans View Their Mental Health* (New York: Basic Books, 1960), p. 403.
11. Haase, W., "Rorschach Diagnosis, Socioeconomic Class, and Examiner Bias" (Unpublished doctoral dissertation, New York University, 1956).
12. Hinsie, L. E., and J. Shatzky, *Psychiatric Dictionary* (New York: Oxford University Press, 1940), p. 284.
13. Hollingshead, A., and F. Redlich, *Social Class and Mental Illness* (New York: John Wiley, 1958), pp. 301, 374, 378, 406.
14. Horney, Karen, *The Neurotic Personality of Our Time* (New York: W. W. Norton, 1937), p. 34.
15. Hunt, R. G., "Social Class and Mental Illness: Some Implications

for Clinical Theory and Practice," *Amer. J. Psychiat.*, 116 (1960), 1065.

16. Joint Commission on Mental Illness and Health, *Action for Mental Health* (New York: Science Editions, 1961), sec. IV.

17. Kinsey, A. C., W. B. Pomeroy, and C. E. Martin, *Sexual Behavior in the Human Male* (Philadelphia: Saunders, 1948), p. 369.

18. Knupfer, G., "Portrait of the Underdog," *Public Opinion Quarterly*, 11 (1947), 103–14.

19. Kohn, M. L., "Social Class and Parent-Child Relationships: An Interpretation," *Amer. J. Sociol.*, 11 (1963), 68.

20. Komarovsky, Mirra, "Blue-collar Families," *Columbia University Forum*, 7:4 (1964), 29–31, 188.

21. Kubie, L., *Practical and Theoretical Aspects of Psychoanalysis* (New York: Praeger, 1960), p. 86.

22. McGuire, C., *Social Status, Peer Status and Social Mobility* (mimeographed; Chicago: Committee on Human Development, University of Chicago, 1948).

23. Merton, R. K., L. Broom, L. S. Cottrell, Jr., *Sociology Today* (New York: Basic Books, 1959), pp. 509–36.

24. Miller, D., and G. Swanson, *Inner Conflict and Defense* (New York: Holt, Rinehart & Winston, 1960), p. 396.

25. Miller, W. B., "Lower Class Culture as a Generating Milieu of Gang Delinquency," *J. Soc. Iss.*, 14 (1958), 5–19.

26. Myers, J. K., and B. H. Roberts, *Family and Class Dynamics in Mental Illness* (New York: John Wiley, 1959), pp. 3, 27, 250.

27. Rieff, R., *New Directions in Mental Health for Labor and Professionals* (mimeographed; New York: National Institute of Labor Education, 1964).

28. ———, and Sylvia Scribner, *Issues in the New National Mental Health Program Relating to Labor and Low Income Groups* (mimeographed; New York: National Institute of Labor Education, 1963), p. 10.

29. Riessman, F., *New Approaches to Mental Health: Treatment for Labor and Low Income Groups*, Report No. 2 (mimeographed; New York: National Institute of Labor Education, 1964), pp. 4, 112.

30. ———, *New Models for a Treatment Approach to Low-Income Clients:* (preliminary mimeographed draft; New York: Mobilization for Youth, 1963), p. 5.

31. ———, and Jean Goldfarb, *Role-Playing and the Poor* (mimeographed; New York: Mobilization for Youth, 1963), p. 4.

32. ———, and Sylvia Scribner, *The Underutilization of Mental Health Services by Workers and Low Income Groups: Causes and Cures* (mimeographed; New York: National Institute of Labor Education, 1964), pp. 3, 10, 12.

33. Roth, I., and R. F. Peck, "Social Class and Social Mobility Factors Related to Marital Adjustment," *Amer. Sociol. Review*, 16:4 (1951).

34. Srole, L., T. S. Langner, S. T. Michael, M. K. Opler, and T. A. C. Rennie, *Mental Health in the Metropolis: The Midtown Manhattan Study* (New York: McGraw-Hill, 1962), vol. I, pp. 249, 395–407.

35. Storrow, H., "Psychiatric Treatment and the Lower-Class Neurotic Patient," *Arch. Gen. Psychiat.*, 6 (1962), 469–77.

36. Stouffer, S. A., E. A. Suchman, L. O. De Vinney, Shirley A. Star,

and R. M. Williams, Jr., *The American Soldier: Adjustment during Army Life* (Princeton, N.J.: Princeton University Press, 1949), vol. I.

37. Sullivan, H. S., *The Interpersonal Theory of Psychiatry* (New York: W. W. Norton, 1953), pp. 367–8.

38. Warner, W. L., R. J. Havighurst, and M. D. Loeb, *Who Shall Be Educated? The Challenge of Unequal Opportunities* (New York: Harper & Row, 1944).

39. ———, and P. S. Lunt, *The Social Life of Modern Community* (New Haven: Yale University Press, 1941), Part IV.

40. ———, Marchia Meeker, and K. Eells, *Social Class in America* (New York: Harper Torchbooks, 1960).

8 ⊚ Social Class, Occupation, and Parental Values: A Cross-National Study

LEONARD I. PEARLIN
MELVIN L. KOHN

In the United States, there is a distinct difference in emphasis between middle and working class parents' values for their children. Middle class parents value self-direction more highly than do working class parents; working class parents emphasize, instead, conformity to external proscription.[1] Self-control is the pivotal parental value for the middle class, obedience for the working class.

One plausible explanation of this difference between middle and working class parental values is that parents of both social classes value for their children the characteristics that seem most appropriate to the conditions of the parents' lives. In particular, class differences in parental values appear to parallel, and may

Reprinted by permission of the authors and publisher from *American Sociological Review*, 31 (August 1966), 466–79. Some of the tables appearing with the original article are not included; interested readers are referred to the above issue of *ASR*.

161

very well be a result of, the characteristically different occupational experiences of middle and working class parents. Self-direction seems more possible and more necessary in middle class occupations; working class occupations allow much less room for, and in fact may penalize, anything other than obedience to rules and directives set down by others. We shall see whether class differences in parental values are due in substantial part to these differences in occupational circumstances.

A logically prior question must first be faced. Is the relationship between social class and parental values limited to the United States, or is it a more general phenomenon? In order to be certain that the relationship is not an artifact of current conditions in the United States, data allowing comparisons through time or across societies are required.[2] For this purpose, we conducted a study in Italy that provides data comparable to those we have for the United States. Italy's historical traditions and many of its contemporary social institutions differ sufficiently from those of the United States to enable us to determine whether the relationship of social class to parental values is limited to the United States or is a more general concomitant of social stratification.

This report, then, considers two central questions:

1. Is social class related to parental values in Italy in much the same way as in the United States—despite all differences in history, culture, and material conditions of life? In particular, is working class parents' high valuation of obedience a result of circumstances peculiar to the United States? Or is the necessity of conforming to external authority so built into the conditions of working class life that even in a different political, economic, and social context, working class parents would have their children learn to conform to external proscription?

2. If social class is similarly related to parental values in the two countries, to what extent is this due to the characteristically different occupational experiences of middle and working class parents? Our earlier American research did not provide the data to pursue this question empirically, but the new inquiry in Italy does.

Tangentially, but hardly incidentally, the present data from Italy give us the opportunity to compare the values of American and Italian parents irrespective of their social class. This is the logical place to begin our inquiry, for we can understand the similarities and differences in the effects that social class may have in the United States and Italy only in the context of a more general understanding of the similarities and differences of the two cultures.

METHODS

The present inquiry, conducted in Turin, Italy, during 1962–63, was designed to be comparble to the study of social class and parent-child relationships we conducted in Washington, D.C., in 1956–57.[3] As in the earlier study, interviews were conducted with approximately equal numbers of middle and working class parents of fifth-grade children. This was accomplished by over-selecting schools known to have a heavy representation of pupils from middle class families. Once the schools were selected, the choice of families was made randomly from the rosters of fifth-grade pupils. Our final sample does not reflect the class distribution of Turin, but the sample from each social class is reasonably representative of that social class.

Letters were sent beforehand to parents chosen for inclusion, informing them of the nature and purpose of the interviews and the sponsorship of the study. Approximately 85 per cent of those contacted participated. Interviews were completed with 861 individuals. Of these, 341 are with fathers and 520 with mothers. The majority, 628, are husband and wife pairs. The interview schedule itself underwent several pretests and revisions.[4] These pretests, coupled with a number of unstructured qualitative interviews, led to the abandonment of some questions and the inclusion of new ones. At the same time, the pretests provided a further training opportunity for the interviewing staff, all of whom had had some previous experience.

A word about Turin. It is the capital city of the Piedmont

region, located in the shadow of the Alps below France. It has long been a principal industrial center. The availability of hydroelectric power has helped make it the fourth largest city of Italy, with a population of over one million. It is economically crucial to the entire country, currently producing 90 per cent of the nation's automobiles and many of its metallurgical and textile products. Historically, it has been an important center of political ferment and activity. Much of the impetus for the reunification of Italy in the middle of the nineteenth century originated in this city; indeed Turin was the first capital of Italy. To this day it has a lively political climate, mirrored by many informal discussion groups in the city's *piazze* as well as by a broad spectrum of trade unions that reflect the principal political currents of the country.

CROSS-NATIONAL COMPARABILITY OF INDICES

In this study, as in cross-national studies generally, the critical methodological problem is to devise indices that measure the same thing in all countries being compared. For the present analysis, it is especially important that our indices of social class and of parental values be as nearly equivalent as possible for the United States and Italy. As it happens, these two concepts require different approaches to the attainment of index equivalence.[5]

There is evidence that all industrialized societies have generally comparable class systems;[6] our observations of an industrialized area of Italy attest to the comparability of its class system to that of the United States. Over-reaching comparability does not necessarily insure the equivalence of indices, however. The problem is to find objective characteristics that indicate essentially the same class position in both countries. Characteristics relevant to class position in one society may be irrelevant in the other and, more problematic, characteristics equally relevant in both countries need not indicate equivalent positions in both. Income and education, for example, are valid indices of social class in both Italy and the United States, but a given amount of either implies higher status in Italy than in the United States. To use such characteristics as indices of class in cross-national comparisons would require the use of a weighted correction.

Occupational prestige is the one characteristic that signifies most closely equivalent class position in the two countries, as well as in most of the rest of the industrialized world. In particular, professionals, managers, proprietors, and white-collar workers have higher class positions in both countries than do foremen, skilled, semi-skilled, and unskilled workers. The location of an individual's occupation within this prestige ranking, therefore, provides us with a basis for determining class position in both societies.

Our sampling procedures in both the United States and Italy were designed to minimize the number of families from the upper and lower extremes of the social class distribution. Since we have largely excluded the upper class extreme, our sample of professionals, managers, proprietors, and white-collar workers comprises a reasonably representative sample of the middle class. Our exclusion of the lower extreme means that our sample of foremen, skilled, semi-skilled, and unskilled workers comprises a reasonably representative sample of the working class. Some intraclass variation is obscured by using only these two broad social class categories, but what is lost in precision is gained in increased cross-national comparability.

Since class position is indicated by an objective characteristic, index equivalence is attained on the basis of *what* information is asked of respondents. Parental values, however, are subjective states; consequently, equivalence lies in the meaning the questions have for the respondents. The achievement of equivalence here depends not only on what questions are asked but even more on *how* they are asked. Essentially, this is a problem of translation. We started with a question that had a demonstrated appropriateness to the American context: From a list of seventeen characteristics derived from extensive interviews, parents were asked to choose the three they considered most important for a boy or girl of their child's age. To use this question in Italy, it was necessary to find expressions that communicate the same meaning as the original seventeen. This was an exacting task that required considerable ingenuity on the part of our Italian colleagues, not to mention the patient help given by a succession of pre-test interviewees.

Along with the problem of equivalence, a second and kindred issue was met: Is the list as exhaustive of the range of parental values for Italians as for Americans? Fortunately for the ease of analysis, the pretests showed that the list is as representative of parental values in Turin as in Washington. This was confirmed by the survey itself: When parents were asked if there were any characteristics not on this list that they considered important, nothing substantively different was suggested.

NATION, CLASS, AND VALUES

Is social class related to parental values in Italy in much the same way as in the United States? The question requires an examination of the relationship of both nationality and class to parental values. The value choices of Italian and American fathers and mothers, separately for the middle and working class of each country, indicate two things: (1) Nationality exerts a profound effect on parental values; (2) despite the considerable difference between Italian and American parental values, social class bears much the same relationship to parental values in both countries.

In some basic respects, the values of Italian and American parents are quite similar. Honesty, for example, is given the highest priority of all the seventeen characteristics in both Italy and the United States. But the rank order of value choices is substantially different in the two countries. Moreover, regardless of social class, American parents are more likely than are Italian parents to value happiness, popularity, and consideration; regardless of social class, Italian parents are more likely than are American parents to value manners, obedience, and seriousness. American parents' values are perhaps more child-centered, emphasizing the child's own development and gratifications, while Italian parental values seem more adult-centered, emphasizing the child's conformity to adult standards.[7]

Despite the differences between Italian and American parental values, almost all of the class relationships noted in the United States are found in Italy too. Of the eight characteristics significantly related to social class in the United States, six are significantly related to social class in Italy, too[8]—obedience and neatness being more highly valued by the working than by the middle class in both countries, self-control, dependability, happiness, and consideration being more highly valued by the middle than by the working class in both countries. In both Italy and the United States, middle class parents are more likely than working class parents to value characteristics that bespeak the child's self-direction, and working class parents are more likely than middle class parents to value characteristics that bespeak his conformity to external proscription.

The *degree* to which social class is related to parental values in either the United States or Italy should not be exaggerated. The rank-order of middle class parents' value choices does not differ greatly from that of working class parents in either country; the difference between the proportions of middle and working class parents who value any given characteristic is never very large. What is impressive is that the relationship of social class to parental values is so very nearly identical in the two countries—this despite the considerable cultural difference between the two.

There are two characteristics, self-control and obedience, that seem to us to embody most clearly the essential difference between the middle class emphasis on self-direction and the working class emphasis on conformity to external proscription. In fact, these two show a *completely* consistent relationship to social class: in both countries, middle class mothers and fathers are significantly more likely than working class mothers and fathers to value self-control, both for sons and for daughters; in both countries, working class mothers and fathers are significantly more likely than middle class mothers and fathers to value obedience, both for sons and for daughters.

It is clear, then, that a high valuation of obedience is not something peculiar to the American working class. On the contrary, obedience is more highly valued by working than by middle class parents in both countries, and by Italians more than by Americans in both classes. The cumulative effect is that Italian working class parents are most apt to value obedience, American middle class parents least so.

And so we have arrived at a rather striking answer to our first question. Not only are the effects of social class much the same in Italy and in the United States; more than that, the conservatism apparent in American working class parental values, far from being a peculiarly American phenomenon, is even more apparent in Italian working class values. It seems the lot of the worker that he must accord respect to authority and teach his children to do so. This is the case with the American worker and even more so with the Italian worker.

THE RELATIONSHIP OF SELF-CONTROL TO OBEDIENCE

Because self-control and obedience most clearly express the essential difference between middle and working class values, and because they are so consistently related to social class in both the United States and Italy, we shall focus all further analyses on these two values. We shall search the different occupational experiences characteristic of the two social classes for a possible explanation of middle class parents' greater valuation of self-control and working class parents' greater valuation of obedience. This requires a closer examination of the two values.

Self-control and obedience would seem to be antithetical values, in that one stresses control from within and the other conformity to external authority. Yet in another respect they are similar: Although they put the locus of control in different places, both stress control. In this respect they stand as one in contrast to such values as, for example, happiness or popularity or being affectionate. It would be well to see to what degree the difference between the two social classes is a matter of a differential valuation of *control,* whatever its source, and to what degree it is a matter of wanting the locus of control to be internal rather than external.

This analysis can be done more precisely with our Italian than with our American data because we secured more information in the Italian study. There we asked parents not only to choose the three most important characteristics from our standard list of seventeen, but also to tell us whether they considered each of the seventeen important or unimportant. This enables us to classify a parent as valuing a particular characteristic *highly* (that is, selecting it as one of the three most important), *moderately* (that is, saying that it is important, but not choosing it as one of the three most important), or *not at all.* With this index, it is possible to see how the valuation of obedience is related to the valuation of self-control. Table 1 presents this for Italian fathers.[9]

For present purposes, there are two basic ways of examining the data of Table 1. The first ignores the source of control, treating self-control and obedience as equally indicative of an emphasis on *control.* It asks, "Are middle class fathers any more or less likely than working class fathers to emphasize control in their values for their children?" Looked at this way, Table 1 shows that virtually identical proportions of middle and working class fathers consider both values very important, one very important and the other moderately important, both moderately important, one moderately important and the other unimportant, or neither even moderately important. The conclusion is unequivocal: class differences in the valuation of self-control and obedience are not at all a result of any differential emphasis on control per se.

The second way of examining the data of Table 1 is to focus on the differential emphasis on internal as opposed to external sources of control, as exemplified by the relative emphasis given to self-control and obedience. This permits us to specify the difference between middle and working class fathers' values more precisely than was possible before. It is not just that working class fathers are more apt to value obedience and middle class fathers self-control. More precisely, although fathers of both social classes are disposed to value obedience, working class fathers are more likely than middle class fathers to value obedience *highly* and *exclusively,* and to regard self-control as altogether unimportant. Middle class fathers are more apt to think that self-control is important. In effect, obedience is valued throughout the culture; what differentiates the middle from the working class is that in the middle class self-control has come to be valued too.

Therefore, we shall array the data so as to highlight the contrast between the valuation of obedience alone and of self-control at all. Table 2 presents the data of Table 1 rearranged to show the basic social class comparison most pointedly. At

TABLE 1: *Distribution of Italian Fathers by Social Class, Valuation of Self-Control, and Valuation of Obedience*

Valuation of Obedience	Valuation of Self-Control			
	Middle Class Fathers			
	Highly	Moderately	Not at all	TOTAL
Highly	7	12	32	51
Moderately	13	29	7	49
Not At All	17	7	43	67
TOTAL	37	48	82	167

Valuation of Obedience	Valuation of Self-Control			
	Working Class Fathers			
	Highly	Moderately	Not at all	TOTAL
Highly	5	18	47	70
Moderately	3	16	14	33
Not At All	8	5	42	55
TOTAL	16	39	103	158

one extreme are the fathers who value self-control highly, followed by those who value self-control moderately. The middle category is comprised of those who attach no value to either. The fourth category is made up of those who value obedience moderately and self-control not at all. The extreme group values obedience highly and self-control not at all. The two classes differ most in the two extreme categories.

In the following analyses we shall combine the five categories into three. Nothing is lost or distorted in thus simplifying the presentation.

THE STRUCTURAL SOURCES OF SELF-DIRECTION IN OCCUPATIONAL EXPERIENCE

We are interested in those dimensions of occupational experience that meet a limited set of conditions: (1) They must be relatively constant aspects of occupation, durable over time,

TABLE 2: *Proportion of Italian Fathers Valuing Self-Control and Obedience, by Social Class*

Valuation of Self-Control and Obedience	Middle Class	Working Class
1. Value self-control highly	.22	.10
2. Value self-control moderately	.29	.25
3. Value neither self-control nor obedience	.26	.26
4. Value obedience moderately and self-control not at all	.04	.09
5. Value obedience highly and self-control not at all	.19	.30
TOTAL	1.00	1.00
Number of cases	167	158
		$\chi^2 = 14.2$, 4 d.f.
		$p < .01$

Source: Table 1.

predictable, and patterned—in short, they must be built into the structure of the occupation; (2) they must differ between middle and working class occupations—for the only dimensions of occupational experience that will help us to explain class differences in parental values are those that are differentially distributed between middle class and working class occupations; (3) they must have *a priori* relevance to the values under scrutiny.

The last is conceptually the most important. Our interest was directed to occupation not only because occupation is so important to social class, but also because we thought that the central difference between middle and working class occupations was precisely what seemed to be at issue in the difference between middle and working class values: "Middle class occupations require a greater degree of self-direction; working class occupations, in larger measure, require that one follow explicit rules set down by someone in authority."[10] Our assumption is that the structural requirements of the job are easily transmuted into personal requirements for doing the job well, and that the characteristics one needs in so major a segment of life as one's occupation come to be valued generally—for oneself, and for one's children as well. In particular, jobs that allow, and require, self-direction should lead to high valuation of self-control; jobs that require following the directions established by someone in authority should lead to high valuation of obedience and low valuation of self-control.

Our task then was to specify and index those dimensions of occupation that meet the above conditions and define the overall occupational situation as conducive to self-direction or to conformity to external direction. There seem to be three such dimensions—the closeness of supervision to which a person is subjected, the principal type of work that he does, and the degree to which the job requires self-reliance. These three are closely related empirically as well as conceptually. But since they are analytically distinct, we shall consider them *seriatim* and only then examine their combined effect.

The Closeness of Supervision

A limiting condition for the exercise of self-direction is the closeness of supervision to which one is subjected. Under conditions of close supervision little leeway is possible. On the other hand, freedom from close supervision, while a condition for self-direction, does not necessarily indicate autonomy. The absence of close supervision might simply indicate a situation where work is so unvaryingly routine that it requires little or no overseeing. In general, however, a situation of close supervision can be taken to mean a limitation on self-direction; we should expect closely-supervised men to be more likely to value obedience and less likely to value self-control for their children than would less closely-supervised men.

We measured closeness of supervision by three questions, which together form a reasonably satisfactory Guttman scale:[11] (1) How much control does your direct supervisor exercise over your work? (2) Do you feel that you are able to make decisions about the things that have true importance to your work? (3) Do you have much influence on the way things go at your work? The scale pattern is such that men who report that their supervisors exert little or no control over them are likely also to claim decision-making power and considerable influence. Those who are unable to exert influence over their work claim little decision-making power and say they are subject to considerable control.

The relationship between supervision and parental values is stronger for the working class, for only in the working class is any considerable proportion of men subjected to very close supervision. Nevertheless, the relationships are essentially the same in the two social classes. The more a man feels he is closely directed from above, the more likely he is to value obedience exclusively. The greater the sense of power a man feels he has over the conditions of his work, the more likely he is to value self-control for his children. The self-employed, who are shown separately, are less likely to value obedience alone, and more likely to value self-control, than are any but the least closely supervised of middle class employees. In sum: In both classes, men who follow orders at work tend to value obedience, those who have greater degrees of freedom in their work situations are more likely to value self-control for their children.

The Principal Component of Work: Things, People, or Ideas

A second dimension of occupation intimately involved in the question of the degree to which one's actions are self-directed is the substance of the work one does. Most working class occupations deal with things, most middle class occupations deal with interpersonal relationships or ideas. Work with "things" typically entails the least freedom for independent judgment, work with "ideas" typically entails the most freedom, even necessity, for independent judgment. The manipulation of ideas is necessarily under more direct control of the individual, while the manipulation of things is more easily standardized and regulated by others. Where the task involves ideas, there is a natural opportunity for autonomy of decision and action.

We asked fathers: "In almost all occupations it is necessary to work with ideas, people, and things, but occupations differ in the extent to which they require these types of activities. Considering now a typical day's work, which of these three aspects of work is most important in your occupation?"

The correspondence between social class and whether one works with things, people, or ideas is close, but, fortunately for analytic purposes, not complete. There are some middle class men who deal principally with things, and some working class men who deal principally with ideas or people. The middle class men who say that *things* are most important to their work are mostly small entrepreneur-craftsmen, dentists, engineers and highly trained technicians, managers and sales personnel whose work is very directly related to the manufacture or distribution of hard goods, and a few clerks whose jobs are so routinized that they see themselves as working with things rather than data. The majority of working class men who say that they work primarily with *people* are in service occupations; the remainder are foremen. Working class men who say that *ideas* are most important to their work are concentrated in highly skilled jobs. What differentiates them from other skilled workers is that their jobs seem to require more independence of judgment or evaluation—as in the case of mechanics who specialize in diagnosis, or testers in the automobile factory. In six cases, however, we have no evidence that the job is substantially different from other working class jobs. Fortunately for the main thrust of our argument, these six men do not account for the relationships we shall present.

The data indicate that men who work mainly with things are the least disposed to value self-control, and that men who work mainly with ideas are the most disposed to value self-control. Obedience is most likely to be stressed by those men, whatever their social class, who work mostly with things. The relationships are strong and consistent in both social classes.

The Requirement of Self-Reliance in Work

The degree of supervision to which a man is subject and the type of work he does put limits on the degree of self-direction a job permits. Within these limits, some jobs in fact *require* that a man make independent judgments, take responsibility, invest himself in his work, while others, although they may permit it, do not actually require it. This is the last aspect of self-direction we wish to index: the degree to which the job *requires* self-reliance.

In the interview, fathers were given a list of qualities and asked to indicate, on the basis of their own occupational experience, the rank order of the three that were most important to doing well at their work. For the remainder they were asked to distinguish between those that were important and unimportant. Four of these items form the dimension "self-reliance." They are: to understand one's self; to be intelligent; to have trust in one's self; and to have a sense of responsibility. The index was formed by giving a weight of four if an item was ranked first in importance, three if it was ranked second, two if it was ranked third, and one if it was considered important even though unranked. These scores were then added for each respondent. Essentially, the higher a man's score, the more his work requires self-reliance.[12] As expected, a man's score on self-reliance is related to his authority situation, and even more closely to whether he works primarily with ideas, people, or things. It follows that degree of self-reliance is also closely related to social class.

The relationship between the degree to which a man feels that his job requires self-reliance and his values for his children is so large that if job and family were not different realms we would suspect it to be merely tautological. Men who think their jobs require a large measure of self-reliance are overwhelmingly more likely to value self-control than are men who do not. Men who think their jobs require little or no self-reliance are overwhelmingly more likely to value obedience.

The Cumulative Effect of All Three Dimensions of Occupation

While closeness of supervision, work task, and the requirement of self-reliance in work are conceptually distinct, they are empirically closely related. It could not be otherwise if occupations were to have structural integrity. Despite their analytical specificity, therefore, it is necessary to examine their interrelationships and their combined effect on parental values.

First, consider whether or not each of the three dimensions of occupation is related to fathers' values independently of each of the other two. Does the need for self-reliance at work affect fathers' valuation of self-control and obedience, for example, regardless of whether the men work primarily with things, with people, or with ideas? The answer, as the data indicate, is yes. In both social classes, regardless of whether men work with things, people, or ideas, those whose jobs require greater self-reliance are more likely to value self-control, while men whose jobs require less self-reliance are more likely to value only obedience. (There are two exceptions, one in each social class.)

The same data show that the effect on parental values of working with things, people, or ideas holds both for men whose jobs require a great deal of self-reliance and for men whose jobs do not. Although there is a close correspondence between working with things, people, or ideas and the degree of self-reliance the job requires, the effects of these two aspects of occupation are both independent and cumulative. Men who work primarily with things on jobs that require little self-reliance are least likely to value self-control and most likely to value obedience alone; at the other extreme, men who work primarily with ideas on jobs that require much self-reliance are most likely to value self-control and least likely to value obedience alone. Comparable tables (not shown here) demonstrate that the effects of closeness of supervision are independent of and additive to each of the other two aspects of occupation.

We cannot extend this analysis to examine the combined effect of all three dimensions of occupation, because that would require a huge number of cases. Fortunately, the question of cumulative effect can be pursued by means of Rosenberg's technique of test factor standardization.[13] This technique allows us to reformulate the question: How much difference would there be between middle and working class fathers' values if their occupational experiences were the same in all three relevant respects?

Table 3 presents the original comparison of middle with working class fathers' values and the same comparison "standardized" on the three aspects of occupational experience. The original difference of 12 per cent in the proportion of men who value self-control *highly* is reduced to 4 per cent. The original difference of 17 per cent in the proportion of men who value self-control *at all* is reduced to zero. In short, the differential occupational experiences of middle and working class men largely account for their differential valuation of self-control.

At the other extreme, the original difference of 13 per cent in the proportion of men who value obedience *highly* is reduced to 1 per cent. Other aspects of social class continue to show some effect, however: The difference in proportions of men who value obedience at least moderately, originally 18 per cent, remains 10 per cent after standardization. Thus the differential occupational experiences of middle and working class men largely account for the difference in the extreme valuation of obedience, but aspects of class not dealt with here still contribute substantially to the greater likelihood over-all of working class men valuing obedience.

Finally, standardization reveals that one effect of social class may be hidden by these three dimensions of occupation. In the original comparison, there is no difference between the proportion of middle and working class fathers who reject both values —who, presumably, do not value control, whatever its source. The standardized comparison suggests that, were it not for these occupational experiences, middle class men would be more likely to reject both values. For many middle class fathers the alternatives are not self-control and obedience; were it not

TABLE 3: *Original and Standardized Proportions of Italian Fathers Valuing Self-Control and Obedience, by Social Class*

Valuation of Self-Control and Obedience	Original Comparison[a]		Standardized Comparison	
	Middle class	Working class	Middle class	Working class
1. Value self-control highly	.23	.11	.18	.14
2. Value self-control moderately	.29	.24	.23	.27
3. Value neither self-control nor obedience	.26	.25	.34	.24
4. Value obedience moderately and self-control not at all	.04	.09	.06	.15
5. Value obedience highly and self-control not at all	.18	.31	.19	.20
TOTAL	1.00	1.00	1.00	1.00
Number of cases	144	141	144	141

[a] The original comparison differs from Table 2, for it excludes those fathers who could not be classified on all three dimensions of occupation.

for their occupational experiences, they would value neither self-control nor obedience, but other characteristics altogether.

SUMMARY AND DISCUSSION

The present inquiry is addressed: (1) to ascertaining whether the relationship of social class to parental values is specific to the United States or is a more general concomitant of social stratification; (2) to determining whether the differences in middle and working class parents' values are due to differences in their occupational conditions.

A cross-national comparison shows that Italian parental values are more adult-centered and American more child-centered. Despite this cultural difference, the relationship of social class to parental values is much the same in both countries. In both Italy and the United States, middle class parents put greater emphasis on the child's self-direction and working class parents on the child's conformity to external proscription. There is something intrinsic to social stratification that yields strikingly similar results in the two countries.

What precisely is it about class that generates differences in parental values? Occupation stands out as a critical dimension of class, especially for men. By occupation we refer to what people do in the course of earning a living and, more pointedly, how the structure of work imposes constraints and imperatives on their behavior. Three features of occupational life, which together define the limits of and demands for the exercise of self-direction at work, were delineated. Each of the three is independently related to fathers' values for their children; their combined effects account for a very large part of the difference between middle and working class fathers' values.

There are four problems which cannot be completely resolved. One problem is the degree to which fathers' occupational experiences affect their *wives'* values. Our data indicate that in middle class families, fathers' occupational experiences are related to their wives' values just as to their own, albeit not quite so strongly. In working class families one can discern a similar relationship, but it is weaker. A more complete explanation of class differences in mothers' values would require further examination of their own experiences.

A second problem is that the relationship between a man's occupational experiences and his values might be due, not to the direct effects of occupational experience, but to those facts that determine what type of occupation he will enter. It is impossible to check all possible relevant facts, but the most important, we think, is education. One would expect more highly educated men to be more likely to work with ideas, to be less subject to supervision, and to need more self-reliance in their work; one would also expect more highly educated men to be more likely to value self-control and less likely to value obedience. In fact, educational level does show a modest relationship to fathers' values. The effect of education is, however, indirect: Education importantly affects occupation, and occupation is of great significance for values. That is, among men of similar occupational circumstances, education is only weakly and inconsistently related to parental values; no matter what their educational level, however, men's values are strikingly and consistently related to their occupational circumstances. Occupation rather than education accounts for virtually all the variation in fathers' values.

A third problem concerns the reciprocity of effect between occupations and values. Although a man's values for his children are hardly likely to affect the conditions of his occupational life, his general value orientation may. There are no data to tell us to what degree the relationship between occupational conditions and parental values is due to the effect of occupation on values, and to what degree it is due to the effect of values on occupation. Given the limited freedom that most men have to decide whether they will be more or less closely supervised, whether they will work with ideas, with people, or with things, and how much self-reliance their jobs will require, it seems probable that the predominant direction of effect is from occupations to values.

Finally, might the close relationship between fathers' occupational experiences and their values for their children indicate that fathers are simply preparing their children for occupational life to come? We believe that more than this is involved, that in a more general and profound way, fathers come to value these characteristics as virtues in their own right and not simply as means to occupational goals. One important piece of evidence buttresses this conclusion: There is exactly the same relationship between fathers' occupational experiences and their values for daughters as for sons, yet in Italy it is hardly likely than any large proportion of the fathers think their daughters will have occupational careers comparable to their own. Occupational experience, we believe, helps structure one's view not only of the occupational world but of the social world generally.

The aspects of occupation we have examined do not completely explain the relationship of social class to parental values. By selecting a critical aspect of social class—occupation—and then selecting critical dimensions of occupation, we have accounted for a large part of this particular social class effect. We would not argue that the same dimensions of class are equally important for explaining all the effects of class. On the contrary, we are convinced that social class is related to so many aspects of behavior because it embraces a number of potent interlocking variables. Occupation is most important in explaining the effect of social class on parental values; education or some other relevant variable may be more important in explaining other effects of class.

REFERENCES

1. See Melvin L. Kohn, "Social Class and Parent-Child Relationships: An Interpretation," *American Journal of Sociology,* 68 (January 1963), 471–80.
2. The only comparative data we have been able to find are very incomplete, but they do support the thesis that in all industrial societies working class parents are more likely than are middle class parents to value obedience in their children. See Alex Inkeles, "Industrial Man: The Relation of Status to Experience, Perception, and

Value," *American Journal of Sociology,* 66 (July 1960), pp. 20–21 and Table 9.

3. For a statement of the design of the earlier study, see Melvin L. Kohn, "Social Class and Parental Values," *American Journal of Sociology,* 64 (January 1959), 337–51.

4. Those parts of the interview schedule that were adopted from American studies were translated by Dr. Pier Brunetti, an American-trained psychiatrist and native of Turin. In addition to translation, Brunetti contributed many substantive suggestions and helped make the many administrative arrangements on which the inquiry depended. The local sponsorship of the investigation was given by the Fondazione Adriano Olivetti, under the direction of Dr. Massimo Fichera. Their logistical support, interest, and encouragement were most generous. We should also like to thank Professor Luciano Saffirio of the University of Turin for his critical reading of the manuscript.

5. We have adopted the term "equivalence" from Almond and Verba, who in their cross-national study of political sentiments encountered the same problem. See Gabriel A. Almond and Sidney Verba, *The Civic Culture: Political Attitudes and Democracy in Five Nations* (Princeton, N.J.: Princeton University Press, 1963), pp. 57–72.

6. Alex Inkeles and Peter H. Rossi, "National Comparisons of Occupational Prestige," *American Journal of Sociology,* 61 (January 1956), pp. 329–339.

7. One other difference between the two countries: In the United States, working class parents are more likely to value certain characteristics for girls and others for boys. Italian parents make virtually no distinction between what is desirable for boys and for girls. In fact, the sex of the child makes no difference for anything we shall discuss in this paper. Thus, for simplicity of presentation, the data will not be presented separately for boys and for girls.

8. The exceptions are curiosity and ability to defend oneself. Middle class American mothers, particularly *upper* middle class American mothers, value curiosity more highly than do working class mothers. Not so in Italy. A problem of language may be at issue, for we could find no Italian word equivalent for "curiosity" which was free of the connotation of voyeurism.

   In the United States, working class fathers are more likely than middle class fathers to value the child's ability to defend himself. In Italy, the middle class is more apt to value the ability to defend oneself. We suspect that in the Italian context, to defend oneself has the connotation, "to be able to take care of oneself in a potentially hostile world."

   Two characteristics are not significantly related to social class in the United States but are in Italy—good manners and being a good student. Both are more highly valued by the working than by the middle class.

9. The picture is essentially the same for Italian mothers; we shall limit ourselves to the fathers because this is more relevant to the subsequent analyses of the effects of various dimensions of occupation on parental values. Too few of the mothers have jobs to permit a systematic analysis of their occupational situations. Later we shall

briefly consider the relevance of fathers' occupational circumstances to their wives' values.

10. Kohn, "Social Class and Parent-Child Relationships: An Interpretation," *op. cit.*, p. 476.
11. Reproducibility = 0.95, Scalability = 0.83.
12. We have some evidence for the unidimensionality of this index: The four items, taken three at a time and dichotomized on the basis of whether or not the attribute is considered important, form quite satisfactory Guttman scales. But the cuttingpoints are such that we cannot use all four items in one scale, and the requirement that we score each item dichotomously (for independence) unduly restricts the power of the index. A simple additive scoring of the four items provides a less elegant but more useful index.
13. Morris Rosenberg, "Test Factor Standardization as a Method of Interpretation," *Social Forces,* 41 (October 1962), 53–61.

Index

185